how2become

Police Officer Exam

www.How2Become.com

Orders: Please contact How2Become Ltd, Suite 14, 50 Churchill Square Business Centre, Kings Hill, Kent ME19 4YU.

You can order through Amazon.co.uk under ISBN 9781912370405, via the website www.How2Become.com, Gardners or Bertrams.

ISBN: 9781912370405

First published in 2018 by How2Become Ltd.

Typeset for How2Become Ltd by Gemma Butler.

Disclaimer

Every effort has been made to ensure that the information contained within this guide is accurate at the time of publication. How2Become Ltd is not responsible for anyone failing any part of any selection process as a result of the information contained within this guide. How2Become Ltd and their authors cannot accept any responsibility for any errors or omissions within this guide, however caused. No responsibility for loss or damage occasioned by any person acting, or refraining from action, as a result of the material in this publication can be accepted by How2Become Ltd.

The information within this guide does not represent the views of any third-party service or organisation.

Fictitious names, faces, characters, businesses, places, events, and incidents in this book are not intended to represent any real individual, company, product, or event. Any resemblance to actual persons, living or dead, or actual events is purely coincidental.

As part of this product you have also received FREE access to online tests that will help you to pass your Police Officer tests.

To gain access, simply go to:

www.PsychometricTestsOnline.co.uk

Get more products for passing any test at:

www.How2Become.com

Contents

INTRODUCTION TO YOUR GUIDE

Welcome to *Police Officer Exam*. In this guide, you'll learn everything you need to know in order to attempt police officer tests in the USA with confidence.

If you're reading this book, then you probably want to become a police officer. In order to do so, you'll need to demonstrate a number of different skills, all of which are essential for working as a member of any police force in America. These tests are designed to assess all sorts of skills, from memory and arithmetic, to visualization and report writing.

To help you prepare for the tests, this book will supply you with sample questions for each type of test or question you might face when applying to become a police officer. These will help you to get used to the style of questions you'll have to answer in the real exams. You'll also have access to explanations for the answers to these questions, so that you can identify where you've succeeded and where you need to improve.

Once you feel comfortable with the format of these questions and how to answer them, you will have access to our mock tests. These are designed to be sat under timed conditions, so that you can experience as true-to-life of a test environment as possible. Once you feel ready, sit the tests in the assigned time-frame. This will give you the best estimate of how well you will perform in the real tests.

Once you've sat the mock tests, take a look at the answers and explanations. These are designed not only to let you know whether your answer is right or wrong, but also to give you an idea of how to improve in the future. Therefore, we recommend sitting one mock test, then checking your answers, before moving onto the next one.

How Should I Use This Book?

As previously mentioned, this book will take you through everything that you need to know in order to apply, study for, and take the police officer tests. Bear in mind that police officer tests are not standardized across the country, which means that some of the questions in this book might not appear in your actual test. For example, some states and counties might place a heavier emphasis on arithmetic tests than others. We recommend that you find out what your area's police tests cover before studying the sample questions in this book.

Likewise, you are most likely aware that different states adhere to different laws. This will also have an impact on that nature of the test, since some types of question require that you understand the laws of the state which you are applying to become a police officer in. While we can't list every single law for every state in the country, we've devoted a chapter of this book to helping you understand the laws for your state. See Chapter 6: Understanding the Law for more information on this.

In this book, you'll also find information on how to apply for police tests, and whether or not you will be eligible for the tests. Again, the precision of this information will depend on your location, and so it is recommended that you check your chosen police force's own eligibility information as well as reading the contents of this book.

The Structure of This Book

This book is divided into the following sections:

Policing in the United States – a summary of the role of a police officer and the police in the United States, as well as an introduction to how the law will differ between states.

The United States Police Tests – what the police tests are, how they are assessed, the tests you are likely to take as a candidate, how to apply for the tests, and whether or not you are eligible to take the tests.

General Studying and Preparation Tips – advice for preparing for any test, with an added focus on studying for your police officer tests.

Police Officer Test Sample Questions – here you will find examples for each kind of question that you might come across in your police officer tests. Answers and explanations will be available for each question.

Exam Tips – advice to take on board for when you take your police officer tests.

Police Officer Mock Tests – sample tests full of questions for you to complete under timed conditions, to get a sense of your progress in preparation for your police officer exams.

The Police Officer Interview – a bonus chapter focusing on interview questions you can expect to be asked in the final interview with the oral interview board, as well as sample responses to help you prepare your own answers for the final interview.

The Aims of This Book

The goal of this book is to prepare you for the police officer exam(s) with as broad a range of potential questions as possible. The exact make-up of your test will depend on the state and even county that you're applying to be a police officer in. For this reason, you will need to conduct your own research on the type of questions you'll be facing in your test, then refer to the appropriate sample questions in this book.

This book is also focused on guiding you through the application process. From finding out whether you are eligible, to tips on how to apply for the test, all the way up to preparing for and taking your test – this book will take you step-by-step through the process of becoming a police officer. With the added bonus chapter focusing on the oral board interview, this book contains everything you need to work your way through an application process, potentially up to your final interview!

POLICING IN THE USA

In order to apply to become a police officer, it's vital that you have an understanding of what the role of a police officer is, as well what the role of police forces in general are. If you're reading this book, then you probably want to become a police officer. This means you probably have a decent idea of what police work involves, as well as some of the values upheld by police

In terms of its legal system, the USA is truly a unique nation. Between federal, state, and county police, and federal and state laws, the legal system in America is complex. Likewise, the United States contains approximately 18,000 different departments, from the highest federal departments all the way down to county and local constabularies. While there are general laws and guidelines that the entire country follows, many states get to make their own decisions about how to police themselves. With a country as huge and diverse as the USA, it makes sense for different states to maintain governance over themselves on a number of issues. This means that, as a police officer, the laws that you enforce will differ from those of an officer in a neighbouring state.

Law enforcement is but one pillar of criminal justice in the United States, working alongside the courts and correctional system (prisons) with the goal of making the country as fair and safe as possible.

The Role of a Police Officer

The role of the police officer is to protect civilians and uphold the law. This could involve anything from ticketing illegally-parked cars and issuing speeding tickets, all the way up to searching for criminals and raiding terror hideouts. While the latter of these are clearly more dangerous than the former, they all play a vital role in making sure that people are protected and are following the law.

The exact role of a police officer heavily depends on the type of police officer that you become. For example, a police officer in vice will focus on crimes involving drugs, prostitution, gambling, and other illegal or regulated substances. Therefore, it's important to know what the different kinds of police officer are.

Types of Police Officer in the USA

Since the USA is such a large and diverse country, there needs to be a vast array of different kinds of law enforcement to tackle any criminal problems the country might face. While this list isn't exhaustive, here are a few different types of police officer that you could become once you've passed the entrance exam and graduated from police academy.

Uniformed Police Officer

This is the quintessential type of law enforcement in the USA. As the name suggests, uniformed police officers complete their day-to-day job in their full police uniform, representing the police force as a whole whilst completing daily activities.

Uniformed police officers will undertake a variety of tasks, from patrolling in specific communities and responding to criminal incidents. However, their role extends to being an active member of the community, getting to know the residents, and providing assistance wherever possible. So, it's quite possible that your job as a uniformed police officer may involve helping elderly residents carry their groceries. While this might not be as action-packed as you were expecting, becoming a trusted member of a community is vital to fully complete the job as it allows you to develop a greater understanding of the people you are protecting.

Generally speaking, graduates from police academy will begin their careers as uniformed police officers. From here, you might get the opportunity to branch out into different roles.

Sheriff

Sheriffs are uniformed like regular uniformed police officers, and complete very similar tasks to them. However, there are a couple of major differences which set sheriffs apart from almost every other kind of police officer:

1. Sheriffs are elected officials – members of the community will vote on a candidate to become a sheriff.

2. Sheriffs and deputy sheriffs also operate on a wider level than uniformed police officers, with a county-wide jurisdiction.

State Police Officer

While most police officers will have a fairly focused jurisdiction, state police officers will be responsible for state-wide issues. Generally speaking, this manifest in the form of patrolling highways, although it does also mean that state police can become involved in investigations if the nature of the investigation stretches beyond the limited jurisdictions of regular police officers.

In addition, state police often help to enforce the law in smaller and rural areas where there might not be a fully-fledged police department.

Detective
Perhaps one of the most recognizable types of law enforcement officer due to their prevalence in fiction, the role of a detective is to investigate crimes. This can involve all kinds of tasks, from examining crime scenes, to questioning witnesses, all the way up to searching for suspects and viewing their interrogations.

Unlike a uniformed police officer, whose job is primarily to prevent crime and protect people, detectives are tasked with solving crimes which have already occurred. Of course, this can lead to protecting people: if you catch a wanted criminal, they won't be able to reoffend because they'll hopefully be in prison.

Generally speaking, police officers expected to work as uniformed officers for a set period of time before they can become detectives. In some departments, detectives will require different qualifications to other kinds of police officer.

Special Jurisdiction Police Officer
This term is used to describe police officers from a range of different specialized jurisdictions. For example, a police officer whose jurisdiction lies primarily in schools is a form of special jurisdiction officer. These officers occupy various different jurisdictions within a police force.

Becoming a Police Officer in the USA

If you want to pass the police officer tests, you'll first need to know what the process of becoming a police officer is. While exact requirements will vary depending on where and when you apply to become a police officer, the following three steps need to be taken:

Graduate from High School with a Diploma or GED
This is the bare minimum requirement in terms of formal education that you will require in order to become a police officer. In addition, certain departments and organizations might require or prefer further qualifications, such as a bachelor's degree.

Pass the Entrance Exam
The entrance exam must be completed before you can attend a police academy and learn how to become a police officer. The entrance exam

will differ depend on where and when you are applying to become a police officer, but will generally assess the following areas:

1. Situational judgement.

2. Arithmetic.

3. Memory.

4. Spatial reasoning.

5. Comprehension.

This book will focus common types of question that appear in police entrance exams, as well as study tips for preparing for them.

Between this stage and the next stage, you might be required to pass an interview. The final chapter of this book is focused on interview tips, as well as sample interview questions and responses to help you prepare.

Complete Police Training
If you are successful in the entrance exam and interview, you will be permitted to begin your training at the police academy. You'll learn everything you need to know in order to begin your career as a police officer.

Other Qualifications

As previously mentioned, some police departments might require more from applicants than the minimum formal requirements. Moreover, if you want to obtain a more advanced position in law enforcement, it would be extremely beneficial to complete at least a bachelor's degree. While a degree in any field will be helpful, Criminology or Forensic Science degrees will serve you extremely well as a police officer who wants to move into more advanced positions.

THE UNITED STATES POLICE TESTS

In this chapter, we'll be taking a look at the basics about what you need to know in order to understand the United States Police test. To do this, we will answer the following questions:

1. What is the United States Police test?

2. What questions am I likely to take?

3. How do I apply for the test?

4. Am I eligible to sit the test?

What is the United States Police Test?

The United States Police test is the entrance exam which all candidates must pass before beginning their training as a police officer at a police academy. The test encompasses a variety of different areas, from situational judgment and memory to math and your understanding of the law. At the time of taking the test, you won't be a trained police officer. So, you aren't expected to understand every single little detail of the law – this is part of what you'll be learning at police academy.

Instead, the entrance exam is used to assess the general skills that you will need in order to become an accomplished police officer. This means that you need to hone your skills in a number of different areas. The sample and mock test questions in this book will help you to improve your ability in all of the key areas that are being assessed by the entrance exam.

As previously mentioned, the exact kind of test questions that you receive, as well as their format, will differ depending on when and where you are taking your entrance exam. Different states, counties, and academies might have their own individual focus when it comes to the tests, and so your test may vary from the exact make-up of this book. However, we've supplied you with a broad range of popular types of question which could appear in your test. Therefore, no matter where you are applying to become a police officer, these questions will still be useful to you.

What Questions am I likely to Take?

As previously mentioned, the exact kind of questions that you are likely to sit will depend on where and when you're applying to become a police officer. The likelihood is that a number of the areas we will discuss in this book will appear in your entrance exam.

However, there is one fact that you can take for granted: the entrance exam will not contain questions which require prior knowledge of the law. For example, you won't need to know the specifics of the difference between battery and assault. All of the information that you need in order to tackle a question which contains the law will be given during the test.

So, this means that what you need to study for during the police officer entrance exam is more skills-based than knowledge-based. Generally speaking, the questions will be written in the context of police and law enforcement scenarios. However, they won't be testing your knowledge of the law.

For example, common memory test questions in the police officer entrance exam will involve reading reports about crimes. For these questions, you'll need to memorise vital information, and then recall the data to answer a series of questions about what you've just read.

How Do I Apply for the Test?

Applying for the police officer entrance exam will differ depending on where and when you're trying to become a police officer. In some cases, you will need to apply for job announcements. You'll then be given a date on which you can take the exam via mail. In other cases, you'll be able to walk into an exam. This, however, is much rarer.

The place to apply for the test will depend on the department that you're applying for. In some cases, it might at the police station itself. Other departments may allow you to apply online. In order to get the most accurate information for your area, we advise that you take a look at the application process on the website of the department to which you are applying.

Am I Eligible to Sit the Test?

The general requirements for becoming a police officer in the United States are:

1. Must be a US Citizen.

2. Must possess a valid driver's license.

3. Must be at least 18 years old (minimum age of 21 in some departments).

4. Must possess a clean criminal record.

In some cases, you may still be eligible even if you possess a criminal record. However, the crimes you committed cannot be major or serious in any way. If you have committed a felony, you will not be eligible to become a police officer.

On top of these requirements, there may be others that you'll need to fulfil. Usually, these will be made clear on the recruitment pages on your department's website. This can include the following:

- Minimum height requirements;

- Eyesight requirements;

- Fees.

GENERAL
STUDYING AND
PREPARATION TIPS

In this chapter, we'll be shifting the focus slightly, and taking a look at other skills and tricks to help you prepare for any exam. These include:

- How to create a revision timetable;

- How to keep yourself motivated;

- How to prevent yourself from becoming distracted;

- How to avoid cramming;

- How to make use of past papers and mark schemes.

Revision Timetables and Planning

Now that you've had the opportunity to explore the different ways of learning, it's time to turn the focus to other general aspects of revision: creating and sticking to a timetable, and making full use of revision materials. Both are extremely valuable when revising, and proper handling of both will improve your grade and make you more likely to score high in exams and in controlled assessments.

The goal of having a revision timetable is to map out all of the work that needs to be done in the time after you've started, up until your exams begin. Your plan doesn't need to be expertly crafted or even particularly nice to look at; it just needs to be clear and easy to read.

The first thing you should do is list every subject that you are taking exams in. Once you've done that, try and find every topic or module within that subject. For the police officer entrance exam, you could use the different types of question as a means of figuring out the areas which you need to learn.

You may wish to go into slightly more detail for each of the topics, but as a foundation, this will be enough to fill in a revision timetable. Do this for every module and for every subject, so that you know roughly how much material there is to cover. It's also worth taking a look at how long each of the chapters for these modules are in your textbook, so that you're aware of any abnormally large or small topics.

Once you've done this, it's time to prioritise all of your subjects and topics. Some people like to rank all their subjects from most important to least important. In other words, it might be worth considering which subjects you find more difficult, and giving them higher priority. If you already feel quite confident about a certain part of your studies, place it slightly lower on your list. This means that the areas that need the most attention will receive it.

Once you've prioritized your subjects, you can also prioritise modules. Bear in mind that a lot of topics in many subjects are cumulative – which means that a good understanding of earlier modules is vital for getting to grips with later ones. This is especially the case with maths and Science, where you're building up knowledge as you go along. For these ones, it's better to start at the beginning and work your way through, but other subjects might allow you to mix things up a bit.

Your timetable should include all of the material that you need to revise outside of school hours. The best way to find out what you need to cover, is to take a look at how the exams divide their content, and then use those to fill the timetable.

How Do I Motivate Myself?

Getting motivated to revise in the first place can be incredibly difficult, and requires a lot of determination and self-control. The earlier you start your revision, the better, but you'll probably be tempted to put off revision: "I'll start next week", or "it's way too early to start revising." Try and start revising 8 weeks before your first exam. This should give you plenty of time to get through all of your topics.

However, even starting the process can be a pain, and when the exams are so far away it's difficult to get the ball rolling. So, you need to motivate yourself to start revising as early and as well as possible. In this section, we'll take a look at some of the ways you can keep yourself motivated and make sure you get through your revision.

Revision Styles

Start by finding revision styles that you actually enjoy. This might sound ridiculous, but if you can find a few techniques that aren't completely unbearable, you'll be more willing to make a start with revision. Remember that you don't have to be constantly doing 'hard revision' such as note-taking. Mix things up and try a number of styles to keep things fresh early on, then maybe move into something more serious later.

Ease Into It

Before you start, revision can feel like a huge mountain, impossible to climb to the top of. It can be incredibly daunting. You might be overwhelmed by the feeling that you are completely unprepared and don't know enough. That said, you need to make a start sometime. Some revision is better than no revision at all, so if you're struggling to get started with your studies, ease your way into it. Start by revising for a much shorter period of time, and maybe focus on the things that you already know well or most enjoy. Once you're comfortable and confident, move onto something that you're less sure of.

Treat Yourself

Make sure you keep yourself motivated with some treats. You don't need to go overboard, but the "carrot and stick" method of revision can keep you working for longer periods of time, allowing you to get through more work. Things like "I'll get some ice cream, but only after I've done the next 3 pages" are a great way of keeping you going and keeping your spirits up.

Think Ahead

Finally, always think ahead past exams. Life continues after your exams. You might feel that you're not in a great place while revising, that your social life is suffering or your free time is being eaten up by studies, but it will all be worth it when you get great results. This positive outlook – thinking towards the future – is one of the best ways to get you started with revision, and keep you going with it too.

Staying Focused

Sometimes, revision can be a total pain, and you'd rather do anything (even sit around doing absolutely nothing!) than open a book and do some hard learning. It's very tempting to procrastinate, but falling into the trap of putting off revision is one of the biggest mistakes you can possibly do.

Here are our top 5 tips for avoiding procrastination and getting on with your work.

Turn Off Distractions

The first thing you should do before starting a revision session is remove any distractions from your workspace. The biggest offenders for causing distractions are games consoles, social media, mobile phones, and of course television. The simple solution to this is to turn off these devices, and put them somewhere out of view or reach, so you aren't tempted to turn them back on and continue texting, messaging or playing games.

Sometimes, however, it isn't practical to move all of these devices. In this case, it's better to find a new workspace, free of electronic devices and other distractions. Many people find that their kitchen or dining room table is an excellent place to study, but find what works best for you and your home. If there's nowhere in your house that's suitable for studying, the local library may be a good choice.

When choosing a place to study, consider the following:

- Is it quiet?

- Are there any gadgets to distract you?

- Will people be walking in and out of the room? Will that distract you?

- Is it comfortable?

- Is there plenty of room for you and all of your notes?

Things get a little trickier when you're using computerised or other online resources such as revision games or podcasts. In these cases, you're going to need your computer, phone or tablet with you, so you'll need to exercise some self-control. Log yourself out of social media if you feel that it's necessary to do so, and make sure to turn off notifications for messaging apps on your phone. You can always take a look during your breaks.

Finally, a few words about listening to music while revising. Be very careful when playing music (especially music with lyrics) while studying. It works for some people, but others will find it incredibly distracting. Experiment with it for yourself, but if you find that it doesn't help you, promptly turn it off.

Give Yourself Plenty of Breaks (but not too many!)

Believe it or not, one of the best ways to avoid procrastination is to take regular breaks. Concentration tends to slide after 45 minutes for a lot of people, so don't push yourself to revise for longer periods of time. If you do this, you'll likely get distracted by almost everything around you, or just get bored or tired. The solution to this problem is to place regular breaks after every chunk of time spent revising. So, if you revise for 45 minutes, you should give yourself a 10 or 15-minute break afterwards. Start with this and then adjust it as necessary, until you get into a routine which is comfortable for you. Remember not to go overboard with breaks. Make sure that you stick to your timetable and routine, so that a 15-minute break doesn't turn into an hour spent watching TV!

Stick to Your Revision Timetable

Writing and filling in a revision timetable is one thing, but it's another thing entirely to stick to it throughout your entire exam season. If it helps, make your timetable more detailed to include breaks and other activities.

It can be tempting to put off revision or bargain with yourself: "I'll only do 2 hours today, but I'll make up for it tomorrow," or "I don't really need to know this stuff, I'll take the rest of the day off." Both of these are risky mind-sets, which don't put you in a great place for succeeding. Good organisation skills come in handy here, and you should try and keep to your timetable as much as possible.

Of course, you can be flexible with your time. Sometimes things come up, and you shouldn't completely sacrifice your social life during the revision period. Just make sure it's reasonable, though.

Make Your Working Environment Comfortable

Outside of keeping things quiet and free from distracting gadgets, you should make sure that your revision space is comfortable enough for you to work in. If the room is too cold or hot, or your chair isn't comfortable to sit on, then you might find yourself not wanting to revise. Make sure your revision space is as comfortable as possible.

Mix Things Up

The final tip for staying focused is to mix things up every so often. One way to do this, is to change the subject that you're revising halfway through the day. This means that you'll still be revising, and you'll keep things fresh. You don't need to switch it up too often, but when you find yourself getting too bored of a topic to continue, finish it and then move onto something else entirely, preferably an area from another subject.

You could also change your revision techniques from time to time, to keep things interesting. If you've spent the whole morning writing notes, why not switch over to a podcast or some learning games? You can refer back to our section on different learning styles to get some ideas on how to make your revision more varied.

Cramming and Why You Should Avoid It

Cramming is the act of trying to stuff in as much revision as possible in the days (or even hours!) just before the exam. It's also possibly the biggest act of sabotage that you can do to yourself.

Cramming happens when a candidate either does very little or no revision before the exams. Before they know it, the exam dates have crept up on them, sending them into a state of panic. These candidates tend to then rush through their textbooks and materials, trying to cover weeks' worth of work in just a few days. In almost every case, this is simply not enough time to adequately revise everything. So, people who cram very rarely benefit from it.

Cramming can actually worsen your performance in an exam. Students who cram often find themselves completely blanking on information when they start answering questions, leaving them helpless during an exam. Cramming doesn't work because you aren't giving your brain enough time to let information sink in.

In an ideal world, you should try to finish your revision for a subject 2 or 3 days before the exam starts. This doesn't always go to plan, but aim to have your revision finished at least 2 days before. Revising the night before an exam is a bad idea, and you should avoid doing so. The day before your exam (and in the hours leading up to it as well) should be spent relaxing and keeping calm, eating well and not allowing yourself to become stressed out by looming thoughts about the test. If you get to the day before your exam and you've finished everything, then you've done an excellent job, and deserve an evening to relax.

POLICE OFFICER TEST SAMPLE QUESTIONS

Now that you've had the opportunity to learn what the police entrance exams are, and learned some top studying tips, it's time to begin to look at sample questions.

In this chapter, we've detailed a collection of popular question types that might appear in your actual police entrance exam. Remember that the exact format of the questions in your entrance exam may differ from those in this book. Therefore, the goal of these questions is not to give you a precise idea of what the questions will look like, but rather help you to familiarise yourself with the style of questions being asked.

The question types covered in this chapter are:

- Arithmetic – Math questions which use problem-solving formats to assess your ability to use operations such as addition, subtraction, multiplication, and division;

- Comprehension – Questions which require the candidate to carefully read and identify key information in a passage, then answer questions based on the information;

- Identify the Perpetrator – Candidates must read the description and details of four cases, and then decide if the suspect in the fourth case should also be considered a suspect in the first three cases;

- Frequency of Information – These questions assess your ability to use probability and knowledge of averages to figure out which answer is most likely to be correct;

- Memory – In these questions, candidates need to memorize an image or passage, and then answer questions using the information that they can recall;

- Patrol Directing – Candidates must read a passage and decide which patrol would be most effective at combatting crime, were the frequency of those patrols increased;

- Police Forms – For this question, candidates must be able to read a passage and figure out which details should appear in different sections of a police report;

- Report Structuring – This type of question requires that you read a series of sentences, and then organise them in a way which makes the most logical sense;

- Sketches – These questions test a candidate's ability to compare sketches of suspects and match them with other potential suspects;

- Wanted Posters – This is a form of memory question which assesses your ability to remember information from a wanted poster and match it to the correct image of a subject;

- Writing Reports – These questions come in two forms. The first tests your ability to identify grammatical, syntactical, and spelling errors by evaluating a series of statements. The second question type assesses how well you can find a suitable re-wording of a report which still represents the important details as accurately as possible.

Arithmetic Questions

The following questions measure your arithmetic skills. You must answer the following arithmetic questions without the aid of a calculator.

Question 1

Mrs May had her apartment broken into twice in the space of six months. The total value of items stolen during the first burglary is as follows:

> 1 diamond necklace = $600.
>
> 2 gold bracelets = $350 each.
>
> 1 ornate vase = $1200.

The total value of items stolen during the second burglary is as follows:

> $1400 in cash = $1400.
>
> 3 dresses = $120 each.

1. What is the total value of the items stolen during the first burglary?

   a. $2300.

   b. $2500.

   c. $2000.

   d. $2550.

2. What is the total value of the items stolen during the second burglary?

   a. $1760.

   b. $1780.

   c. $1750.

   d. $1700.

3. What is the total difference in value between the two burglaries?

   a. 700.

b. 720.

c. 740.

d. 750.

Question 2

A raid on a notorious gang hideout resulted in the 33rd Precinct seizing a large number of weapons:

17 handguns.

5 automatic rifles.

12 shotguns.

4 hatchets.

7 machetes.

On top of this, fifteen gang members were arrested.

1. How many weapons were seized in total?

a. 43.

b. 45.

c. 41.

d. 46.

2. How many firearms were seized?

a. 33.

b. 32.

c. 35.

d. 34.

3. What was the ratio of weapons seized to gang members arrested?

   a. 4:1.

   b. 3:1.

   c. 45:15.

   d. 2:1.

Question 3

In the last three weeks, the 20th Precinct has gathered the following crime statistics:

     4 burglaries

     17 assaults

     2 armed robberies

     1 homicide

     7 arsons

1. How many crimes were recorded in total?

   a. 30.

   b. 31.

   c. 32.

   d. 29.

2. How many more assaults were committed than burglaries?

   a. 12.

   b. 10.

   c. 13.

   d. 14.

3. Excluding arson and burglary, how many crimes were recorded?

    a. 24.

    b. 27.

    c. 20.

    d. 19.

Comprehension Questions

Question 1

Read the following passage carefully, then answer the proceeding four questions on the following pages, based solely on the information in the passage.

Police Officers Rockwell and Graves were working their 7am to 3pm patrol shift on Friday, March 23. At 11:30am, they received instructions from the radio dispatcher to respond to a robbery on 52nd Street. As they arrived at the scene of the crime, they found Tariq Anderson, a 20-year-old Asian male. Tariq was the victim of the robbery, as he'd had his backpack stolen. Tariq had called 911 on his cell phone after the thief had stolen the bag. The bag had contained his laptop, Law textbooks, and a lunchbox.

Tariq had been walking to college for a class at 12:00pm, when he had stopped for a moment to tie up his shoelaces. He removed his backpack from his back before kneeling down to tie up the laces on his sneakers, when the thief ran past, grabbed the bag, and then turned left on the corner at the end of the block. Tariq attempted to chase the thief, but with his shoelaces untied, he tripped over and was unable to continue running. It was at this point that he called 911.

After taking a report from Tariq, officers Rockwell and Graves began to ask potential witnesses on the street if they had seen anything, such as a local shopkeeper, John Redman. Mr Redman said he had not seen the robbery take place, but said he had witnessed a similar incident at around midday two days before. Graves and Rockwell could not find any evidence that this previous crime had been reported, but Mr Redman insisted that he had seen a white male in a blue, hooded sweater steal a handbag from a lady as she stopped to cross at the lights. After conferring with Tariq, he said that he remembered that the person who robbed him was also wearing a blue hoodie.

1. Which of the following items was **not** in Tariq's backpack?

    a. Laptop.

    b. Cell phone.

    c. Lunchbox.

    d. Textbooks.

2. On which day had Mr Redman witnessed a woman having her handbag stolen?

    a. Wednesday.

    b. Thursday.

    c. Saturday.

    d. Monday.

3. At approximately what time had Tariq been robbed at?

    a. 11:00am.

    b. 10:30am.

    c. 12:00pm.

    d. 11:30am.

4. Which of the following is true about the previous crime that Mr Redman mentioned?

    a. It occurred on the same day as the crime Officers Rockwell and Graves were responding to.

    b. The crime had happened at night.

    c. There were no witnesses.

    d. The crime had not been reported.

Question 2

Read the following passage carefully, then answer the proceeding four questions on the following pages, based solely on the information in the passage.

At 10:30pm, while on a shift from 9:00pm to 5:00am, Police Officers Phelps and Danton were called to respond to a burglary on 91 33rd Street. The building in question was an apartment building, and the victim was Martha May, a 65-year-old white female. Mrs May, a widow, lives alone on the 3rd floor of the building, in apartment 36.

Upon arrival, Officers Phelps and Danton realised that the main door to the building had not been broken into. Rather, it appears that it had been left open accidentally. One of the witnesses, a resident in the building, remarked that the main door was often left wide open. When asked, Mrs May said she had never noticed the door being left open at night, since she was rarely outside after 7:00pm.

Mrs May stated that she had been in her neighbour's apartment, belonging to an Angela Weissman, when the burglary occurred. She left her apartment at 7:30pm, and had returned at 10:15pm to find that her apartment had been broken into. It appeared as though someone had forced the door open. The possessions stolen included a diamond necklace, three silver bracelets, $200 in cash, and an antique vase. Mrs May declared that she did not care for any of the stolen possessions, apart from the vase – it had been a gift from her recently deceased mother-in-law. Mrs May had not seen anyone enter or leave her apartment – she only witnessed the aftermath.

Officer Phelps asked Mrs May's neighbours to see if they had witnessed anything. One resident, a 55-year-old Hispanic male, stated that he saw a white woman, approximately in her thirties or forties, blonde hair, and around 5'4", hanging around on the third floor of the building earlier that day. However, he did not witness her attempting to break into Mrs May's apartment. The investigation is ongoing.

1. Which of the following statements is true about the woman that was spotted in the apartment building?

    a. She was Hispanic.

    b. She had black hair.

    c. She was in her twenties.

    d. She had been on the same floor as Mrs May's apartment.

2. During what window of time could the burglary have taken place in?

    a. 8:00pm-11:00pm.

    b. 7:30pm-10:15pm.

    c. 7:30pm-9:00pm.

    d. 7:30pm-8:30pm.

3. Which floor had the burglary taken place on?

    a. The first floor.

    b. The second floor.

    c. The third floor.

    d. The fourth floor.

4. At this point in the investigation, which of the following details about the white female suspect is least likely to be accurate?

    a. Gender.

    b. Hair Colour.

    c. Height.

    d. Age.

Question 3

Read the following passage carefully, then answer the proceeding four questions on the following pages, based solely on the information in the passage.

At 3:30pm, during a 9:00am to 6:00pm shift, Police Officers Ramirez and Jackson were called to the scene of a hit and run incident on the corner of 9th Street. They arrived at the scene of the crime at 3:35pm, alongside an ambulance which was treating injuries. There were two victims of the crime: a 33-year-old black female, and a 26-year-old black male. According to the paramedics at the scene, neither had suffered life-threatening injuries, although the female had been taken to hospital to be treated for what appear to be a broken leg. The male was being treated on-site for apparent concussion and minor bruising on the torso.

The male victim, Zackary Andrews, stated that the car that had hit him was a silver sedan. However, he didn't get a chance to read the number plate. Mr Andrews says that he was hit by the car whilst crossing at traffic lights. The lights were red, and pedestrians were signalled to cross. While crossing, Mr Andrews and the other victim were hit by the car, which then proceeded to speed off. All the other witnesses were able to verify that the car was a silver sedan, but no-one was able to read the license plate. All of the witnesses confirmed that the lights were red, and that the pedestrians were being signalled to cross.

Officers Ramirez and Jackson headed to the hospital where the female victim was being treated for a broken leg. The woman, Dana Roberts, had been treated with painkillers in the hospital to ease the pain in her leg. She claimed to have seen nothing, but seemed to agree that the car was silver. She did not get a look at the driver of the vehicle.

1. How long did it take for the officers to arrive at the scene of the crime?

    a. 15 minutes.

    b. 7 minutes.

    c. 5 minutes.

    d. 10 minutes.

2. Which of the following is most likely to have caused the hit and run incident?

    a. Drunk-driving.

    b. Running a red light.

    c. Speeding.

    d. Jay-walking.

3. Which of the following details about the driver was confirmed by witnesses?

    a. They were male.

    b. They were white.

    c. They were wearing a suit.

    d. None of the above.

4. What injury, or injuries, had Mr Andrews suffered?

    a. Concussion and minor bruising on the torso.

    b. A broken leg.

    c. A broken arm.

    d. A broken leg and concussion.

Identify the Perpetrator Questions

For the following questions, you need to read the four incidents carefully. You then need to decide, based purely on the information in these incidents, whether the perpetrator in Incident 4 can also be considered a suspect in Incidents 1, 2, and/or 3.

Question 1

The 99th Precinct has been receiving reports and complaints of an individual, or individuals, driving up and down Darcy Boulevard and 13th Street, playing extremely loud and offensive music throughout the night. Witnesses and victims have been able to give their descriptions in three of these incidents:

Incident 1

Time and Date of Occurrence: 11:30pm on Thursday, March 1, 2018.

Place of Occurrence: Darcy Boulevard.

Suspect Description: White male, early twenties, wearing a red cap and black puffer jacket. Suspect had pock-marked face, and drove a black sedan with a dent in the front passenger door.

Other Details: Music described as 'gangster rap'.

Incident 2

Time and Date of Occurrence: 1:45am on Monday, March 5, 2018.

Place of Occurrence: Darcy Boulevard.

Suspect Description: Black male, early thirties, wearing a dark red t-shirt and gray beanie hat. Suspect was wearing glasses, and drove a black sedan.

Other Details: None.

Incident 3

Time and Date of Occurrence: 2am on Friday, March 9, 2018.

Place of Occurrence: 13th Street.

Suspect Description: White male, early forties, wearing a green parka jacket. Suspect was driving a silver sedan.

Other Details: None.

The 99th Precinct was able to make an arrest on a perpetrator playing extremely loud music out of their car:

Incident 4

Time and Date of Occurrence: 2am on Friday, March 9, 2018.

Place of Occurrence: Darcy Boulevard.

Suspect Description: White male, early forties, wearing a white t-shirt. Suspect was driving a silver sedan.

Other Details: None.

The arrested person in Incident 4 can also be considered a suspect in which of the following?

a. Incident 1 and Incident 3, not Incident 2.

b. Incident 2, not Incident 1 or Incident 3.

c. Incident 1, not Incident 2 or 3.

d. None of the incidents.

Question 2

The 10th Precinct has been attempting to tackle incidents of drug distribution in high schools over the past three weeks. In three of these incidents, witnesses were able to give the following information on suspects:

Incident 1

Time and Date of Occurrence: 8:45am on Thursday, April 19, 2018.

Place of Occurrence: St. Peter's High School – parking lot.

Suspect Description: White male, 5'9", late twenties, 160 pounds. The suspect was bald, clean-shaven, and wore a camo-print hooded jacket and gray jeans.

Other Details: Suspect distributed drugs in aluminum foil wrapping.

Incident 2

Time and Date of Occurrence: 3:35pm on Tuesday, April 24, 2018.

Place of Occurrence: Lone Valley High – behind sports facilities.

Suspect Description: Hispanic female, 5'4", early twenties, 130 pounds. The suspect had dark brown hair, and wore a black track suit with white sneakers.

Other Details: None.

Incident 3

Time and Date of Occurrence: 4:20pm on Wednesday, April 25, 2018.

Place of Occurrence: St. Peter's High School – parking lot.

Suspect Description: White male, 5'9", late twenties, 160 pounds. The suspect was bald, and wore a black cap, khaki cargo shorts, and a gray t-shirt.

Other Details: None.

Two days after Incident 3 took place, Police Officer Bourne made an arrest on an individual attempting to trespass onto school property. They were found to be carrying marijuana.

Incident 4

Time and Date of Occurrence: 9:15am on Friday, April 27, 2018.

Place of Occurrence: Lone Valley High – at fence around the perimeter of the school.

Suspect Description: White male, 5'9", late twenties, 160 pounds. Bald, wearing a red t-shirt and blue jeans.

Other Details: Was carrying marijuana.

The arrested person in Incident 4 can also be considered a suspect in which of the following?

a. Incident 1 and 3, not Incident 2.

b. Incident 1, not Incident 2 or 3.

c. Incident 3, not Incident 1 or 2.

d. None of the incidents.

Question 3

The 140th Precinct is attempting to tackle a recent rise in extortion in stores along 12th Street. Victims and witnesses of three incidents were able to give the following descriptions of the perpetrators:

Incident 1

Time and Date of Occurrence: 6:15pm on Wednesday, January 3, 2018.

Place of Occurrence: Marlow's Groceries, 12th Street.

Suspect Description: Black male, 6'0", 180 pounds, wearing a hooded sweater, black ballcap, and raw denim jeans. Had a tattoo of a revolver on his neck.

Other Details: Suspect demanded that the cashier pay 'protection money', smashed a window, and then left with money that the cashier gave to him.

Incident 2

Time and Date of Occurrence: 8:15pm on Saturday, January 6, 2018.

Place of Occurrence: Benny's Pizza, 12th Street.

Suspect Description: White male, 5'10", 160 pounds, wearing a leather jacket, black jeans, and black boots. Long beard, shoulder-length hair.

Other Details: Used a crowbar to threaten the owner of the restaurant, until the owner turned over a bag of money.

Incident 3

Time and Date of Occurrence: 3:40pm on Saturday, January 6, 2018.

Place of Occurrence: Nancy's Boutique, 12th Street.

Suspect Description: White male, 6'0", 180 pounds, wearing a black suit. Clean-shaven, short brown hair.

Other Details: Grabbed a member of staff by the collar and threatened to punch them unless they handed money over to them.

Some time after these incidents took place, police responded to an attempted extortion on 12th Street. The description was as follows:

Incident 4

Time and Date of Occurrence: 4:10pm on Monday January 8, 2018.

Place of Occurrence: Benny's Pizza, 12th Street.

Suspect Description: White male, 5'11", 150 pounds, wearing a black t-shirt and track pants. Clean-shaven, bald.

Other Details: Drew a handgun during the extortion, demanding that the owner pay protection money.

The arrested person in Incident 4 can also be considered a suspect in which of the following?

a. Incident 1 and Incident 3, not Incident 2.

b. Incidents 1, 2, and 3.

c. Incident 3, not Incidents 1 or 2.

d. None of the incidents.

Frequency of Information Questions

For the following questions, you need to use your understanding of probability to find the correct answers. You might also need to use some outside knowledge to find the correct answer.

Read the following passages, and then choose the correct answer based on the information in the text, as well as what is most likely to be true.

Question 1

An assault took place inside a hair salon in the 33rd Precinct. There are four witnesses, all of which give a different description of the perpetrator. Which of the following descriptions is most likely to be correct?

a. Male, white, 20 years old, 6'5", black suit, brown eyes.

b. Female, white, 30 years old, 5'3", leopard-print jumpsuit, brown eyes.

c. Female, white, 30 years old, 5'3", white t-shirt and black jeans, brown eyes.

d. Female, white, 30 years old, 5'3", white t-shirt and black jeans, blue eyes.

Question 2

A car larceny took place in a blue-collar neighborhood within the 4th Precinct. Four witnesses were questioned, and all gave varying descriptions of the stolen vehicle. Which of the following descriptions is most likely to be correct?

a. Black SUV, area license plate.

b. White sportscar, area license plate.

c. Black SUV, foreign license plate.

d. Black sedan, area license plate.

Question 3

An armed robbery took place inside a jewelry store. Four witnesses gave their account of what weapon was used by the perpetrator. Which of the following descriptions is most likely to be correct?

a. Machete.

b. Shotgun.

c. Handgun.

d. Rifle.

Memory Questions

Part 1

For the following question, you will be given a sketch of an area to examine. You have two minutes to study the image, and commit as much information to memory as possible. You should try to focus on any information that might be important, such as license plates on vehicles, names of places, and other details which might seem important.

Once this two-minute period has elapsed, turn over to the following page and answer the questions based on what you can remember about the image. At this point, you cannot look back at the image.

1. There is a man running from the entrance of the store towards the gas station forecourt. What is he holding in his hand?

   a. Car keys.

   b. Briefcase.

   c. Shopping bag.

   d. Wallet.

2. How many vehicles are on the gas station forecourt?

   a. 2.

   b. 4.

   c. 6.

   d. 1.

3. How many people are standing on the sidewalk by the entrance to the store?

   a. 3.

   b. 2.

   c. 4.

   d. 1.

4. How many vehicles are waiting to use the center gas pump?

   a. 1.

   b. 3.

   c. 4.

   d. 0.

Part 2

For the following questions, you will be given an extended passage to read. You have ten minutes to read the passage, and commit as much information to memory as possible. Your goal is to focus on the most important information, such as names, dates, times, and other details about the crime. Once you have spent ten minutes reading the text, turn the page and begin to answer the questions based on the information you can recall about the passage. Once you have turned over, you cannot return to re-read the passage.

Question 1

At 9:33pm, on Monday February 20, 2017, Officers Hale and O'Hara were called to the scene of a robbery at a jewelry store on Buchanan Street. The crime was reported by Bartholomew King, a resident in the apartment block across the road from the jewelry store. The owner of the store, Ms Mary Hathaway, lives outside of town, and therefore was not immediately aware of the robbery.

At the scene, Officers Hale and O'Hara discovered that the left-most window at the front of the store had been completely shattered. The central window had also been shattered. Mr King said that he had heard gun-shots, which suggests that the window had been shattered using a firearm. The two officers called for back-up as they believed the suspect to be armed.

Back-up arrived in the form of three more officers. Including Officers Hale and O'Hara, four of the officers were armed with handguns, whilst one was armed with a shotgun. The five proceeded to move into and through the store until they found one man with his back to the front of the store where the officers entered from. The suspect was unlocking display cases, scooping up necklaces, and then throwing them into a black bag. While doing this, the suspect had left his firearm on a display cabinet about 12 feet away from him, and it was far out of reach for him to grab quickly.

The officers were able to approach the suspect and arrest him for armed robbery. He was then taken to the 12th Precinct to be processed.

1. Which of the store's windows had been shattered?

   a. Left-most.

   b. Left-most and central.

   c. Right-most and central.

   d. All of them.

2. Approximately how far away from the suspect was his firearm?

   a. 3 feet.

   b. 5 feet.

   c. 10 feet.

   d. 12 feet.

3. How many officers were at the scene in total?

   a. 5.

   b. 3.

   c. 4.

   d. 7.

4. What was the suspect putting into his black bag?

   a. Rings.

   b. Necklaces.

   c. Bracelets.

   d. Watches.

Question 2

In the space of a week, there had been three different cases of carjacking in the 93rd Precinct. This was an unusual frequency, but there was no significant connection between the three occurrences.

The first carjacking occurred on the corner of 23rd and 24th Street, at 11:30pm on July 9 2017. The suspect is an Asian female, approximately in her twenties, wearing a black cap and black puffer jacket. The vehicle stolen was a black SUV. The victim was a black woman who lived three blocks away from where the carjacking occurred. There were two witnesses who confirmed the suspect's appearance, as well as the appearance of the car. Neither of them could confirm her approximate height.

The second carjacking occurred on Vine Street at 7:05pm on July 11 2017. The suspect is a white male with dark brown hair. He was wearing a light-wash denim jacket, dark jeans, and a pair of suede boots. The vehicle stolen was a silver sedan, which can easily be identified by a number of dents in the passenger door. The victim was a white male, 45 years old, who had been driving home from work. No other witnesses have come forward.

The third carjacking was witnessed by three people. It occurred at 12:10pm on July 13 2017. The location of occurrence was 10th Street. The vehicle stolen was a red sportscar. The victim was an Asian female, 25 years old, who was driving to a nearby restaurant to meet with her partner. The suspect was a Hispanic female, in her thirties, wearing a grey parka jacket and dark grey jeans.

1. Which of the carjackings had three witnesses?

   a. The first carjacking.

   b. The second carjacking.

   c. The third carjacking.

   d. None of the above.

2. What time did the second carjacking take place at?

   a. 7:00pm.

   b. 11:30pm.

   c. 12:15am.

   d. 7:05pm.

3. What shoes was the suspect in the second carjacking wearing?

   a. Suede boots.

   b. Black sneakers.

   c. Dress shoes.

   d. Sandals.

4. What type of car was **not** stolen in any of the three carjackings?

   a. Silver sedan.

   b. Black SUV.

   c. Silver SUV.

   d. Red sportscar.

Question 3

Police officers Torres and Davidson were interviewing a witness of an armed robbery of an electronics store on Main Street at 3:15pm. The witness, a black male in his forties, had watched from across the road as a white male and a black male had stood outside the store. The white male discharged his weapon into the air outside, before the two rushed into the store. Amidst the chaos of people running away, the pair of them appeared to punch a security guard in the face, before smashing display cases containing electronic goods such as laptops and headphones.

After approximately thirty seconds, the two males emerged from the front of the building, each carrying goods taken from the store. The white male was carrying headphones, two laptops, and a portable speaker system. The black male was carrying three laptops. The white male had dark brown hair, and was wearing a white t-shirt and black sweatpants. The black male was wearing a red shirt, partially buttoned up, as well as blue jeans.

As they left the building, a black sedan screeched down the road and stopped in front of the electronics store. Both men climbed into the back seats of the car as it sped off. The witness could not recall the appearance of the driver.

1. What was the white male carrying as he left the store?

  a. Three laptops.

  b. One laptop.

  c. Three laptops, a pair of headphones, and a portable speaker system.

  d. Two laptops, a pair of headphones, and a portable speaker system.

2. What time did the armed robbery occur at?

  a. 3:00pm.

  b. 2:15pm.

  c. 3:15pm.

  d. 3:00am.

3. What color was the black male's shirt?

  a. Black.

  b. White.

  c. Blue.

  d. Red.

4. How old was the witness?

  a. In his forties.

  b. In his fifties.

  c. In his thirties.

  d. In his twenties.

Patrol Directing Questions

For this section, read the information in each paragraph. Then, answer the three questions based purely on the information in the paragraph.

Question 1

The 19th Precinct are reviewing crime statistics over the past year in order to figure out what the force could be doing to reduce crime in the area. Crime statistics gathered over the past year have demonstrated that carjackings most often occur between 8pm and midnight, and are more likely to occur on 16th Street. Most of the burglaries occurred on Thursday nights. Unsurprisingly, most instances of shoplifting occurred during the daytime from 10am-3pm. However, it was discovered that shoplifting most often occurs on Mondays.

1. In order to reduce the number of carjackings in the precinct, what would be the most effective patrol?

   a. 8pm-11pm on Thursday nights.

   b. 8pm-1am every night.

   c. 8pm-12am every night.

   d. 8pm-12pm every night.

2. In order to reduce the frequency of shoplifting, what is the most effective day to patrol?

   a. Thursday.

   b. Monday.

   c. Saturday.

   d. Friday.

3. In order to reduce the number of burglaries, what is the most effective day to patrol?

   a. Monday.

   b. Sunday.

   c. Friday.

   d. Thursday.

Question 2

Crime statistics for the 76th Precinct demonstrated a number of facts about crime in the area. Firstly, the statistics showed that homicides most often occurred between 1am and 3am on Saturday and Sunday mornings. Homicides were also least likely to occur between 9am and 11am on Mondays, Tuesdays, and Wednesdays. In contrast, assaults were most frequent between 8pm and midnight every night. Finally, it was found that car larceny occurred most commonly at night, between 7pm and 10pm.

1. In order to reduce the number of homicides, which would be the best patrol to increase?

   a. 1am to 3am on Saturday mornings.

   b. 1am to 3am on Friday mornings.

   c. 1am to 3am on Saturday and Sunday mornings.

   d. 9am to 11am on Mondays, Tuesdays, and Wednesdays.

2. In order to reduce the frequency of car larceny, which of the following patrols would be the best to focus on?

   a. 7am to 10am.

   b. 7am to 10pm.

   c. 7pm to 10pm.

   d. 10am to 7pm.

3. In order to reduce the number of assaults, which of the following patrols would be the best to increase?

   a. 8pm to midnight.

   b. 8am to midday.

   c. 8pm to 1am.

   d. Midnight to 8am.

Question 3

Officers working in the 26th Precinct were analysing crime statistics from the previous three years. The officers found that the distribution of illegal drugs most often occurred on Friday and Saturday nights. Distribution of marijuana was most common between 6pm and 8pm on Friday and Saturday nights, whilst distribution of cocaine was most frequent between 11pm on Friday and Saturday nights and 1am on Saturday and Sunday mornings. Opioids, whether legal or illegal, were found to be distributed between 10pm on Friday and Saturday nights and 4am on Saturday and Sunday mornings. Opioid-related distribution offences accounted for 70% of drug offenses in this period.

1. Which of the following patrols would be most effective for reducing marijuana distribution?

   a. 6pm to 11pm on Friday and Saturday nights.

   b. 8pm to 11pm on Friday and Saturday nights.

   c. 11pm to 1am on Friday and Saturday nights.

   d. 6pm to 8pm on Friday and Saturday nights.

2. Which of the following patrols would be most effective for reducing cocaine distribution?

   a. 11pm on Friday and Saturday nights, to 1am on Saturday and Sunday mornings.

   b. 10pm on Friday and Saturday nights, to 1am on Saturday and Sunday mornings.

   c. 11pm on Thursday and Friday nights, to 1am on Friday and Saturday mornings.

   d. Midnight on Friday and Saturday nights, to 3am on Saturday and Sunday mornings.

3. Which of the following patrols would be most effective for reducing the frequency of drug offenses overall?

a. 6pm to 2am every night.

b. 10pm on Friday and Saturday nights, to 4am on Saturday and Sunday mornings.

c. 6pm to 8pm on Friday and Saturday nights.

d. 6pm to 8pm on Saturday and Sunday nights.

Police Forms Questions

Question 1

For the following question, read the passage in relation to the blank arrest report. Then, answer the four questions on the following pages.

On Monday, October 23, 2017, Officers Anita Davis (shield #1129) and Joseph Matthews (shield #2872) were on a 3pm-10pm patrol. Two hours and fifteen minutes into their patrol, they were called to the scene of a brawl outside of a liquor store on 29th Street.

Upon arrival five minutes later, Officers Davis and Matthews observed four men fighting, seemingly in two pairs. One pair consisted of Johnny Dixon – a 26-year-old white male who is known by the police force, and Tom Alvarez – a 24-year-old Hispanic male. The other pair contained two white males: Al Rider, 35 years old, and his cousin, Colin Rider, 32 years old.

At the scene, Officers Davis and Matthews observed Mr Al Rider punch Mr Alvarez in the gut, and then again in the face. In retaliation, Mr Dixon grabbed Mr Al Rider and proceeded to put him in a headlock. Mr Alvarez then began to punch Mr Al Rider in the ribs. It was at this point where Officers Davis and Matthews were able to break up the fight. Officer Davis then proceeded to arrest all four of the men for assault. While arresting Mr Dixon, it was apparent that he was carrying a large knife, which he had not drawn.

Mr Alvarez received arrest #4592, Mr Al Rider received arrest #4593, Mr Colin Rider received arrest #4594, and Mr Dixon received arrest #4595. Detective Chad Stone (shield #1249) of the assault investigations team, was assigned to the investigation.

Arrest Report

Person(s) Arrested

(1a) Name:

(1b) Charge:

(1c) Description of Arrestee:

(1d) Arrest Number:

(2a) Name:

(2b) Charge:

(2c) Description of Arrestee:

(2d) Arrest Number:

(3) Time and Date of Occurrence (24-hour clock):

(3a) Place of Occurrence:

(4) Details of Offense:

(5) Place of Arrest:

(6) Time and Date of Arrest (24-hour clock):

(7) Description of Property Vouchered:

(7a) Voucher Number:

(8) Name of Arresting Officer:

(8a) Shield Number:

(9) Assignment of Arresting Officer:

(10) Detective Assigned for Follow-Up Investigation (name, shield number, assignment):

1. Which of the following should be entered into field (3)?

    a. 1700, Monday, October 23, 2017.

    b. 1715, Monday, October 23, 2017.

    c. 5:15pm, Monday, October 23, 2017.

    d. 5:30pm, Monday, October 23, 2017.

2. Which of the following should be entered into field (8a)?

    a. #1129.

    b. #4592.

    c. #4594.

    d. #2872.

3. Which of the following should be entered into field (10)?

    a. Detective Chad Stone, #1129, Assault Investigations Team.

    b. Detective Chad Stone, #1249, Assault Investigations Team.

    c. Officer Anita Davis, #1129, Assault Investigations Team.

    d. Detective Anita Davis, #1129, Assault Investigations Team.

4. Which of the following should be entered into field (5)?

    a. Liquor store on 23rd Street.

    b. Liquor store on 25th Street.

    c. Strip mall on 23rd Street.

    d. Liquor store on 29th Street.

Question 2

For the following question, carefully read the information in the arrest report. Then, answer the questions based purely on the information in the report.

Arrest Report

Person(s) Arrested

(1a) Name: Kiera Jackson.

(1b) Charge: Breaking and entering.

(1c) Description of Arrestee: Hispanic female, brown hair, brown eyes, 5'6", 21 years old. Wearing a black hooded sweater, black sweatpants, and gray sneakers.

(1d) Arrest Number: #3561.

(3) Time and Date of Occurrence (24-hour clock): 0300.

(3a) Place of Occurrence: 106 Canal Street.

(4) Details of Offense: Suspect broke into the music store at 106 Canal Street by smashing a window. Suspect attempted to steal an electric guitar worth approximately $600. Police were called after owner heard the window smashing.

(5) Place of Arrest: 106 Canal Street.

(6) Time and Date of Arrest (24-hour clock): 0315.

(7) Name of Arresting Officer: Officer Jack Brady.

(7a) Shield Number: #4331.

(8) Detective Assigned for Follow-Up Investigation (name, shield number, assignment): Detective Marcos Pizjuán, #1074, Burglary.

1. The person who called the police is:

    a. Someone who witnessed the crime.

    b. The owner of the music store.

    c. A concerned neighbour.

    d. A security guard at the store.

2. The time taken between the incident occurring and an arrest being made was:

    a. Twenty minutes.

    b. Ten minutes.

    c. Fifteen minutes.

    d. Eight minutes.

3. The suspect is:

    a. Black.

    b. White.

    c. Asian.

    d. Hispanic.

4. The shield number of the arresting officer is:

    a. #1074.

    b. #3561.

    c. #0315.

    d. #4331.

Question 3

For the following question, read the passage in relation to the blank arrest report. Then, answer the four questions on the following pages.

At 8:30pm on Wednesday, February 8 2017, Clarissa Burton attacked her sister, Carrie, at Carrie's home on 30 Vale Street. In the living room, Clarissa and Carrie had got into an argument about Carrie's husband, Peter. Carrie accused Clarissa of having an affair with Peter, to which Clarissa responded that Peter has been 'sleeping with every woman in this town'. Carrie proceeded to use offensive language towards Clarissa.

In retaliation, Clarissa attacked Carrie with her bare hands, punching her in the stomach and tripping her over. While Carrie was lying on the floor, Clarissa ran into the kitchen, grabbed a knife, and returned to the living room to continue attacking Carrie.

It was at this point that Peter entered the house, and immediately dialled 911 as he saw Clarissa approach Carrie with a knife. Peter shouted for Clarissa to put the knife back in the kitchen. Clarissa dropped the knife and ran upstairs crying. Peter then moved to help Carrie off of the floor.

Officers Jane Roland (shield #1674) and Mickey Smith (shield #1855) arrived at the house at 8:45pm. Officer Roland went upstairs to arrest Clarissa, whilst Officer Smith proceeded to question Carrie and Peter. While Carrie was not badly wounded, an ambulance was called to ensure that the punches to her stomach and her fall had not caused any damage.

Officer Roland arrested Clarissa for assault at 8:48pm. Clarissa received arrest #6143 and was taken to the 112th Precinct to be processed. The knife, while not used in the assault, was vouchered under #1180. Detective Patrick McCabe (shield #5684), assault unit, was assigned to the investigation.

Arrest Report

Person(s) Arrested

(1a) Name:

(1b) Charge:

(1c) Description of Arrestee:

(1d) Arrest Number:

(2) Time and Date of Occurrence (24-hour clock):

(2a) Place of Occurrence:

(3) Details of Offense:

(4) Place of Arrest:

(5) Time and Date of Arrest (24-hour clock):

(6) Description of Property Vouchered:

(6a) Voucher Number:

(7) Name of Arresting Officer:

(7a) Shield Number:

(8) Assignment of Arresting Officer:

(9) Detective Assigned for Follow-Up Investigation (name, shield number, assignment):

1. What information should be entered into field (1b)?

    a. Battery.

    b. Attempted murder.

    c. Assault.

    d. Aggravated assault.

2. What information should appear in field (5)?

    a. 2048, February 8 2017.

    b. 1848, February 8 2017.

    c. 2045, February 8 2017.

    d. 2030, February 8 2017.

3. What information should appear in field (7a)?

    a. #1855.

    b. #5684.

    c. #1674.

    d. #1574.

4. What information should appear in field (6)?

    a. Knife.

    b. Hatchet.

    c. Handgun.

    d. Crowbar.

Report-Structuring Questions

For these questions, read the information in each passage. Then choose the most logical order for the information to appear in if you were writing a report.

Question 1

Police Officer Peña is writing a report concerning vandalism. Her report consists of the following five sentences:

1. I discovered a group of young men throwing rocks through a shop window.

2. I arrived at the scene 5 minutes after receiving a signal from the dispatcher.

3. Most of the young men ran off when the police car arrived, although we were able to apprehend one of them.

4. I received a call from the dispatcher requesting a response to vandalism on 27th Street at 7:35pm.

5. Myself and my partner took the individual into custody and returned them to the station, arriving at approximately 7:55pm.

Which order of the above sentences makes the most logical sense?

a. 4, 1, 2, 3, 5

b. 4, 2, 1, 3, 5

c. 1, 3, 5, 2, 4

d. 4, 5, 1, 3, 2

Question 2

Detective Lynn Taylor has just finished interrogating a suspected drug dealer. She is preparing a report based on the interrogation. Her report consists of the following five sentences:

1. The suspect leaned back in their chair and refused to answer my question.

2. As I entered the room, the suspect immediately declared that they wanted a lawyer before proceeding.

3. I advised the suspect of his rights after sitting down at the table in the interrogation room.

4. I then asked the suspect where they were at 11:15pm the night before, where an individual who matches his description had been seen distributing illegal drugs.

5. I asked two more questions, but the suspect refused to answer either of them.

Which order of the above sentences makes the most logical sense?

   a. 2, 3, 4, 1, 5

   b. 3, 2, 4, 1, 5

   c. 2, 3, 1, 4, 5

   d. 3, 2, 5, 1, 4

Question 3

Police Officer Plumber is preparing a report concerning a DUI (driving under the influence) arrest he made earlier that evening. His report consists of the following five sentences:

1. I signalled for the driver to pull over where it was safe for him to do so.

2. I placed the driver under arrest and drove him to the station so that he could be processed.

3. I performed a breathalyzer test to confirm that he was over the legal alcohol limit for driving.

4. While driving, I noticed a black SUV swerving in the road.

5. I followed the SUV to see if the driver would continue to swerve or otherwise lose control of the vehicle.

Which order of the above sentences makes the most logical sense?

a. 4, 1, 5, 3, 2

b. 4, 1, 5, 2, 3

c. 4, 5, 1, 2, 3

d. 4, 5, 1, 3, 2

Sketches Questions

For the following question, you need to examine the face of the suspect. Then, you need to decide which of the other faces, if any, match the face of the initial suspect. For this exercise, assume that the suspect has not undertaken any reconstructive surgery.

SUSPECT

FACE 1   FACE 2   FACE 3

Which of the faces match the suspect?

   a. None of them.

   b. Face 1.

   c. Face 2.

   d. Face 3.

Wanted Poster Questions

For the following question type, you need to closely read and examine the four wanted posters over the next four pages. This is a form of memory test, so you will need to memorize the details of the images as well as the information beneath them. You have five minutes to read and examine all four of the wanted posters.

Once five minutes have passed, turn over and answer the questions based purely on the information that you have remembered from the wanted posters. You need to match the correct subject's image to the details in each question.

Subject 1

WANTED FOR RACKETEERING & ARSON

Andrés Torres

Age: 24.

Race: Hispanic.

Sex: Male.

Height: 6'2".

Weight: 170 pounds.

Eye Color: Brown.

Hair: Dark Brown.

Tattoo(s): Christian cross on back of neck.

Scars: None.

Subject is part of a gang which offers 'protection' to markets and vendors in the 44th Precinct. Subject is known for setting property on fire when protection money is not presented. Subject also known for spending his racketeering money at local strip clubs.

Subject 2

WANTED FOR MURDER

Willow Peterson

Age: 30

Eye Color: Brown.

Race: White.

Hair: Brown.

Sex: Female.

Tattoo(s): None.

Height: 5'4".

Scars: None.

Weight: 125 pounds.

Subject wanted for the murder of her partner two weeks prior. Subject is believed to be travelling with her three-year-old son. Subject murdered her partner using a semi-automatic rifle. It is believed that this weapon is still in her possession. Subject drives a gray SUV.

Subject 3

WANTED FOR ASSAULT

Vincent Smith

Age: 50

Race: White.

Sex: Male.

Height: 5'11"

Weight: 185 pounds.

Eye Color: Green.

Hair: Brown.

Tattoo(s): Anchor on left bicep.

Scars: Straight scar over lip.

Subject is wanted for assaulting a black male in a bar on 34th Street. Subject is known for being verbally abusive towards black people in the past. During the assault, subject repeatedly used racial slurs. Assault is considered to be racially motivated.

Subject 4

WANTED FOR FRAUD

Franklin Johnson

Age: 28

Eye Color: Brown.

Race: Black.

Hair: Brown

Height: 5'9".

Tattoo(s): None.

Weight: 170 pounds.

Scars: None.

Subject convinces acquaintances at bars and clubs to make exorbitant bets, and then rigs the bet in his own favour. Subject often uses card games when defrauding a victim. Subject is believed to have defrauded over $10,000 in cash and belongings.

1. Which of the following subjects is travelling with their three-year-old son?

   a. Subject One.

   b. Subject Two.

   c. Subject Three.

   d. Subject Four.

2. Which of the following subjects uses card games when defrauding victims?

   a. Subject One.

   b. Subject Two.

   c. Subject Three.

   d. Subject Four.

3. Which of the following subjects frequently spends their money in strip clubs?

   a. Subject One.

   b. Subject Two.

   c. Subject Three.

   d. Subject Four.

4. Which of the following subjects has a tattoo of an anchor?

   a. Subject One.

   b. Subject Two.

   c. Subject Three.

   d. Subject Four.

Writing Reports Questions

Part 1

For each of the following questions, you will be given a series of three statements. Your task is to read each statement and decide on whether or not they are grammatically accurate, clearly-written, and free from spelling errors. Choose the statement which is the most accurate and well-written (i.e. the one which has no grammar or spelling errors). If you believe that none or all of the statements have these errors, then choose option D.

Question 1

Evaluate the following statements:

a. The driver swerves then drove through the fence.

b. The witness stated that he was to tired to focus.

c. The perpetrater jumped onto the train just as it was leaving.

d. All or none of the above are accurate.

Question 2

Evaluate the following statements:

a. The arrest was made quick.

b. The Officer spent a long time in the building.

c. There was no people in the house.

d. All or none of the above are accurate.

Question 3

Evaluate the following statements:

a. There tyres had been slashed.

b. The dog had barked all morning.

c. There where no signs of forced entry.

d. All or none of the above are accurate.

Part 2

For each of the following questions, you will be given a series of information about a case. Once you've read it, choose the paragraph from the answer options which most accurately represents the information in the initial passage.

Question 1

Detective Liza Harper has gathered the following facts during her investigation:

Place of Occurrence	Micah's Barbers, 42 107th Street
Time of Occurrence	3:35pm
Time of Reporting	3:40pm, by one of the barbers
Crime	Assault
Victim(s)	Male, black, 45 years old
Suspect	Male, Asian, 20 years old
Weapon	Fists, metal baseball bat

Which of the following paragraphs best represents the above information?

a. An Asian male, 20 years old, assaulted a 45-year-old black male at Micah's Barbers (42 107th Street) at 3:35pm. The suspect used both his fists and a metal baseball bat during the assault. The crime was reported by the victim.

b. An Asian male, 20 years old, assaulted a 45-year-old black male at Micah's Barbers (42 107th Street) at 3:35pm. The suspect used both his fists and a metal baseball bat during the assault. The crime was reported by one of the barbers working at the barbershop.

c. A black male, 20 years old, assaulted a 45-year-old black male at Micah's Barbers (42 107th Street) at 3:40pm. The suspect used both his fists and a metal baseball bat during the assault. The crime was reported by one of the barbers working at the barbershop.

d. An Asian male, 20 years old, assaulted a 45-year-old black male at Micah's Barbers (42 107th Street) at 3:40pm. The suspect used his fists during the assault. The crime was reported by one of the barbers working at the barbershop.

Question 2

After arriving at the scene of a crime, Detective Vincent Johnson gathers the following information:

Place of Occurrence	Parking lot of Peak Valley business park.
Time of Occurrence	11:30am
Time of Reporting	3:00pm
Crime	Car Theft
Victim(s)	White male, 33 years old
Suspect	Unknown white male

Which of the following paragraphs best represents the above information?

a. At approximately 3:00pm, an unknown white male broke into and stole a car from the parking lot of the Peak Valley business park. The car belonged to a 33-year-old white male.

b. At approximately 11:30am, an unknown white male broke into and stole a car from the parking lot of the Peak Valley business park. The car belonged to a 33-year-old white male.

c. At approximately 11:30am, an unknown white male stole a car from the parking lot of the Peak Valley business park. The car belonged to a 33-year-old white male.

d. At approximately 11:30am, an unknown white male stole a car from outside the victim's house. The car belonged to a 33-year-old white male.

Question 3

Detective Maria Henderson arrived at a crime scene and obtained the following information:

Place of Occurrence	Maude's Bar, 23 12th Street
Time of Occurrence	11:15pm
Time of Reporting	11:20pm
Crime	Vandalism
Victim(s)	Owners of Maude's Bar
Suspect	White female, 23 years old

Which of the following paragraphs best represents the above information?

a. At 11:20pm, a 23-year-old white female was spotted vandalising across the road from Maude's Bar (23, 12th Street). The crime was reported at 11:20pm.

b. At 11:15pm, a 23-year-old white female was spotted vandalising across the road from Maude's Bar (23, 12th Street). The crime was reported at 11:20pm.

c. At 11:15pm, a 23-year-old white male was spotted vandalising Maude's Bar (23, 12th Street). The crime was reported at 11:20pm.

d. At 11:15pm, a 23-year-old white female was spotted vandalising Maude's Bar (23, 12th Street). The crime was reported at 11:20pm.

Police Officer Test Sample Questions – Answers and Explanations

Arithmetic Questions

Question 1

1. b = $2500.

   Explanation = $600 for the diamond necklace, plus $350 each gold bracelet ($700), plus $1200 for the ornate vase.

   $600 + $700 + $1200 = $2500.

2. a = $1760.

   Explanation = $1400 in cash, plus $120 for each of the three dresses ($360).

   $1400 + $360 = $1760.

3. c = $740.

   Explanation = $2500 from the first burglary minus $1760 from the second burglary.

   $2500 - $1760 = $740.

Question 2

1. b = 45.

   Explanation = This is the sum of all of the weapons.

   17 + 5 + 12 + 4 + 7 = 45.

2. d = 34.

   Explanation = This is the sum of all weapons (45), minus the hatchets and machetes (11).

$45 - 11 = 34$.

3. b = 3:1.

    Explanation = To solve the ratio, divide the number of weapons seized (45) and the number of gang members arrested (15) by the highest common factor. In this case, the highest common factor is 15, and so 45 and 15 are divided by 15.

    $45 \div 15 = 3$

    $15 \div 15 = 1$.

    3:1.

Question 3

1. b = 31.

    Explanation = This is the sum of all of the recorded crimes

    $4 + 17 + 2 + 1 + 7 = 31$.

2. c = 13.

    Explanation = Subtract the number of burglaries (4) from the number of assaults (17).

    $17 - 4 = 13$.

3. c = 20.

    Explanation = Take the total number of crimes (31), then subtract the number of arsons (7) and burglaries (4) from it.

    $31 - 7 = 24 - 4 = 20$.

Tips for Answering Arithmetic Questions

- While it might look complex, the problem-solving in this type of question essentially boils down to straight-forward mathematics;

- Don't get too wrapped up in the contextual details of the question, unless the answer strictly requires you to. Instead, focus on the numbers which you need to deal with;

- For any math question, make sure that you remember the order of operations (also known as BODMAS). The order is as follows:

Brackets (or Parentheses)	Solve any sums which are in brackets first.
Orders (or powers of e.g. squared, cubed, square root)	Any orders or powers of need to be solved after brackets.
Division	Division needs to be solved after orders.
Multiplication	Multiplication comes after division.
Addition	Addition sums need to be resolved after multiplication.
Subtraction	Finally, complete any subtraction operations within the problem.

- While these questions aren't too difficult once you get the hang of them, it's important that you double-check all of your answers. Once you arrive at your answer, quickly complete it again to ensure that you haven't made a mistake in your calculations;

- If your answer doesn't match any of the answer options, then you've definitely made a mistake somewhere. Go back through your calculations and try to figure out where you went wrong.

Comprehension Questions

Question 1

1. b = Cell phone.

   Explanation = The final line of the first paragraph states that the bag contained Tariq's laptop, Law textbooks, and lunchbox. Therefore, the only answer option left is his cell phone.

2. a = Wednesday.

   Explanation = This incident has occurred on Friday. On the same day, officers Rockwell and Graves questioned Mr Redman as a witness. Mr Redman states that he had seen a similar incident occur two days before. Two days prior to Friday is Wednesday.

3. d = 11:30am.

   Explanation = Officers Rockwell and Graves received the call from the dispatcher at 11:30am. Therefore, it is fair to assume that the incident occurred at approximately 11:30am.

4. d = The crime had not been reported.

   Explanation = In the final paragraph, it is made clear that Rockwell and Graves could find no evidence that the crime had been reported. Therefore, one has to assume that the crime was not reported.

Question 2

1. d = She had been on the same floor as Mrs May's apartment.

   Explanation = The woman in question was described to be white, with blonde hair, and in her thirties or forties. Therefore, she was not Hispanic, had black hair, or was in her twenties. By process of elimination, this leaves answer option D.

2. b = 7:30pm-10:15pm.

   Explanation = Mrs May returned to her apartment to find it had been robbed at 10:15pm. She left her apartment at 7:30pm earlier that evening. Therefore, the largest possible window is between 7:30pm and 10:15pm.

3. c = The third floor.

   Explanation = Mrs May lives on the 3rd floor of the building. The burglary occurred at her apartment. Therefore, the burglary took place on the third floor of the building.

4. c = Height.

   Explanation = Judging someone's height to an exact degree just from looking at them is extremely difficult, especially for a witness who just spotted the person. Whilst hair colour, gender, and age can be approximated with greater precision more easily, height can be difficult to determine. Therefore, height is the least likely piece of information to be true.

Question 3

1. c = 5 minutes.

   Explanation = Officers Ramirez and Jackson received the call at 3:30pm. They arrived at the scene at 3:35pm. Therefore, it took them five minutes to respond to the call and arrive at the scene of the crime.

2. b = Running a red light.

   Explanation = If the victims were pedestrians who were hit as they were crossing at traffic lights, then it most likely that the incident occurred because the driver was running a red light. In addition, all of the witnesses confirmed that the lights were red and that pedestrians were signalled to cross, meaning that the pedestrians were not jay-walking.

3. d = None of the above.

   Explanation = Neither the witnesses nor the victims were able to recall any details about the driver.

4. a = Concussion and minor bruising on the torso.

   Explanation = The first paragraph confirms that the male victim, Mr Andrews, was7 being treated for apparent concussion and minor bruising on the torso.

Tips for Answering Comprehension Questions

- These questions require a significant level of attention to detail. You will need to carefully read through the passage, possibly multiple times, before reaching the correct answer;

- Read the passage at least once before even looking at the questions. Then, once you've read the questions, re-read the passage looking for information which helps you to answer them;

- If you're allowed to, and if it helps, you can underline or highlight any details which you might believe are important. This will make it easier to find key information without having to search through the entire passage;

- Read the questions and answer options carefully. The answer might seem obvious, but that's possibly a red herring being used to trick you;

- Some answers might be plain to see in the text, whilst others may require closer attention to detail and even some reading between the lines may be necessary.

Identify the Perpetrator Questions

Question 1

d = None of the incidents.

Explanation = While the suspect in Incident 4 matches the description of the suspect in Incident 3, both incidents occurred at the same time. Therefore, the perpetrator in Incident 4 could not be considered for Incident 3. Likewise, Incidents 1 and 2's descriptions do not match the description of Incident 4. Therefore, the perpetrator of Incident 4 cannot be considered a suspect

Question 2

a = Incident 1 and 3, not Incident 2.

Explanation = The description of the suspect in Incidents 1 and 3 match the description in Incident 4. Since the dates and times of the incidents do not contradict each other, the perpetrator in Incident 4 should be considered in Incidents 1 and 3.

Question 3

d = None of the incidents.

Explanation = The description of the perpetrator in Incident 4 does not match the description in Incidents 1, 2, or 3. Therefore, the perpetrator of Incident 4 cannot be considered a suspect in the other incidents.

Tips for Answering Identify the Perpetrator Questions

- These questions will test your ability to identify key information and compare it to other data. Therefore, it's important that you constantly cross-reference the details of each incident;

- Keep a close eye on the times and dates of the incidents, since they might affect your answer. For example, if Incident 1 and Incident 4 both occur at the same time but in different places, it's almost certain that the suspect of Incident 4 can't also be a suspect in Incident 1. After all, someone can't be in two places at once;

- Take note of each suspect's appearance, as well as details which may change between incidents. For example, the suspect of Incident 1 might have a beard, but in Incident 3 they might not. However, it's entirely possible that the suspect shaved. The same can be considered for hair styles and clothing. In cases where incidents are taking place far apart from one another, the suspects' weight might even change;

- Other key details, such as murder weapons, might also hint at a suspect being considered in more than one Incident. If the details are particularly unusual, then this can be a key indicator as to whether a suspect in one incident should be considered for another;

Frequency of Information Questions

Question 1

c = Female, white, 30 years old, 5'3", white t-shirt and black jeans, brown eyes.

Explanation = Brown eyes are more common than blue eyes, which makes option C more likely than option D. The outfit of a white t-shirt and black jeans is more common than a leopard-print jumpsuit, making it more likely than option B. If three of the witnesses state that the suspect is a female, then it is more likely that the witness is a female.

Question 2

d = Black sedan, area license plate.

Explanation = Since this is a blue-collar neighbourhood, it's not likely that there would be a white sportscar present. This eliminates option B. It's also more likely that the car has an area license plate than a foreign one, which eliminates option C. Finally, sedans are generally more common than SUVs, eliminating option A. This leaves option D.

Question 3

c = Handgun.

Explanation = Of all of these weapons, handguns are the most readily available. Likewise, due to their simplicity and size, they are most likely to be used during a robbery.

Tips for Answering Frequency of Information Questions

- These questions require some kind of prior knowledge about the world. Essentially, you need to be able to identify what is most likely to be the case;

- Sometimes, this will be simple. For example sedans are more common than sportscars. This means that it's more likely that a sedan was involved in a traffic collision than a sportscar, simply due to the fact that there are more sedans on the road than sportscars;

- In some cases, you might need to think more carefully. Brown eyes are more common than blue eyes, so it's more likely that the suspect had brown eyes;

- In some cases, you might need to look at the actual content of the answer options. For example, if three witnesses state that the suspect is male, and one witness states that the suspect was female, it's more likely that the suspect was male;

- When preparing for this question, it helps to have a good idea about demographics and appearances. For example, it's helpful to know that the average height of males in the USA is 5'10". Therefore, if the suspect is a man, it's more likely that he is 5'10" than 5'3". Study what the averages are for all kinds of data in the country, and you should be well-equipped to answer this kind of question.

Memory Questions

Part 1

1. c = Shopping bag.

    Explanation = The man running towards the forecourt has a small, white shopping bag in his left hand.

2. b = 4.

    Explanation = While there are six vehicles in the entire image, only four of them on the forecourt.

3. b = 2.

    Explanation = There are two people standing right outside of the entrance to the store, on the sidewalk.

4. a = 1.

    Explanation = Only one car can be seen waiting behind the vehicle which is at the gas pump in the center lane of the forecourt.

Part 2

Question 1

1. b = Left-most and central.

    Explanation = The beginning of the second paragraph details that the left-most and central windows had both been shattered.

2. d = 12 feet.

    Explanation = The final sentence of the third paragraph states that the suspect had left his firearm on a display cabinet about 12 feet away from him.

3. a = 5.

    Explanation = Two officers were at the scene at the start of the passage. The first sentence of the third paragraph states that back-up arrived in the form of three more officers. This comes to a total of five officers.

4. b = Necklaces.

    Explanation = The third paragraph details that the suspect was unlocking display cases and scooping up necklaces.

Question 2

1. c = The third carjacking.

    Explanation = The first sentence of the final paragraph states that the third carjacking was witnessed by three people.

2. d = 7:05pm.

    Explanation = The first sentence of the third paragraph details that the second carjacking occurred at 7:05pm.

3. a = Suede boots.

    Explanation = In the third paragraph, the suspect is described to be wearing a pair of suede boots.

4. c = Silver SUV.

    Explanation = The vehicle stolen in the first carjacking was a black SUV. The vehicle stolen in the second carjacking was a silver sedan. The vehicle stolen in the third carjacking was a red sportscar. Therefore, the only vehicle in the answer options which was *not* stolen in the three carjackings.

Question 3

1. d = Two laptops, a pair of headphones, and a portable speaker system.

   Explanation = The second paragraph states that these were the items that the white male was carrying.

2. c = 3:15pm.

   Explanation = The first paragraph states that the armed robbery took place at 3:15pm.

3. d = Red.

   Explanation = The final sentence of the second paragraph states that the black male was wearing a red shirt.

4. a = In his forties.

   Explanation = The first paragraph states that the witness was a black male in his forties.

Tips for Answering Memory Questions

- The memory questions are quite similar to the comprehension questions we took a look at earlier. Your task remains the same: identify key details and then use them to answer the questions;

- However, this time you'll need to be able to remember the key details, since you aren't allowed to re-read the passage or look at the image once you've started on the answer questions;

- You won't be allowed to take any notes on this section, so it's important that you remember details in your head. Some people find that the best way to do this is to read the information, divide it into small chunks, and then remember each piece. So, if you need to remember a telephone number, you can break it up into lots of small groups of numbers, and then remember those. This can work for other pieces of information as well;

- Since you don't get a second chance to re-read the information, it might be worth guessing the answer if you have no chance of remembering it. Choose the answer which seems most likely to you, and move onto the next question. There's no point staring at a question hoping that it will jog your memory if nothing's coming to mind.

Patrol Directing Questions

Question 1

1. c = 8pm-12am every night.

   Explanation = The passage states that carjackings most often occur between 8pm and midnight. No specific days of the week are specified. Therefore, the best patrol to increase would be 8pm-12am every night.

2. b = Monday.

   Explanation = Shoplifting occurs most often on Mondays. Therefore, increasing patrols on Monday would be most effective.

3. d = Thursday.

   Explanation = Burglaries occurred most often on Thursday nights. Therefore, the most effective day to patrol on is Thursday.

Question 2

1. c = 1am to 3am on Saturday and Sunday mornings.

   Explanation = The statistics show that homicides were most likely to occur between 1am and 3am on Saturday and Sunday mornings. Therefore, increasing patrols during this time would be most effective for reducing homicides.

2. c = 7pm to 10pm.

   Explanation = Car larcenies occurred most often between 7pm and 10pm. Therefore, increasing patrols during this time period would be most effective.

3. a = 8pm to midnight.

   Explanation = Assaults occurred most frequently between 8pm and midnight every night. Therefore, increasing patrols between 8pm and midnight would be most effective.

Question 3

1. d = 6pm to 8pm on Friday and Saturday nights.

   Explanation = Marijuana distribution is most frequent between 6pm and 8pm on Friday and Saturday nights. Therefore, increasing patrols during this time would be most effective for reducing marijuana distribution.

2. a = 11pm on Friday and Saturday nights, to 1am on Saturday and Sunday mornings.

   Explanation = Cocaine distribution occurs most commonly between 11pm on Friday and Saturday nights, to 1am on Saturday and Sunday mornings.

3. b = 10pm on Friday and Saturday nights, to 4am on Saturday and Sunday mornings.

   Explanation = Opioid distribution accounts for 70% of all drug offenses. Therefore, in order to have the largest impact on drug distribution, it makes the most sense to focus on opioid distribution. Opioid distribution is most common between 10pm on Friday and Saturday nights, to 4am on Saturday and Sunday mornings. Therefore, it makes the most sense to increase patrols during this period.

Tips for Answering Patrol Directing Questions

- This question type essentially boils down to comprehension. You need to carefully read the information in the passage, especially the times and places where different crimes are most likely to occur;

- Keep track of which crimes occur at which places and times. For example, if the text says muggings occur most often on Saturday nights between 9pm and 11pm, then either highlight it or make a note of it;

- Sometimes, the questions may ask you to think a bit more about the best patrol to increase. The passage might discuss different kinds of drugs and when they are most commonly distributed, but the question might ask you generally which patrol should be used to combat the distribution of drugs in general. In this case, you'll need to pool all of the information from the passage in order to choose the correct answer.

Police Forms Questions

Question 1

1. b = 1715, Monday, October 23, 2017.

   Explanation = Field (3) concerns time and date of occurrence. The time of the incident was two hours and fifteen minutes into their patrol, which makes 5:15pm (1715). The date is confirmed to be Monday, October 23, 2017.

2. a = #1129.

   Explanation = Field (8a) concerns the shield number of the arresting officer. The arresting officer was Officer Anita Davis, whose shield number is #1129.

3. b = Detective Chad Stone, #1249, Assault Investigations Team.

   Explanation = Field (10) concerns the details of the detective leading the follow-up investigation. Detective Chad Stone, #1249, Assault Investigations Team, is the detective leading the follow-up investigation.

4. d = Liquor store on 29th Street.

   Explanation = Field (5) concerns the place of arrest, which was a liquor store on 29th Street.

Question 2

1. b = The owner of the music store.

   Explanation = Field (4) reads that the owner of the music store heard the window smashing, and then called the police.

2. c = Fifteen minutes.

   Explanation = Field (3) shows that the crime occurred at 0300. Field (6) shows that the time of arrest was 0315. Therefore, it took fifteen minutes for the arrest to be made after the incident occurred.

3. d = Hispanic.

   Explanation = Field (1c), Description of Arrestee, lists the suspects ethnicity as Hispanic.

4. d = #4331.

Explanation = Field (7a) contains the shield number of the arresting officer. This field contains #4331.

Question 3

1. c = Assault.

Explanation = The suspect was arrested for assault. Therefore, the charge in this field should be assault.

2. a = 2048.

Explanation = Field (5) concerns the time and date of arrest. The arrest occurred at 2048, February 8 2017.

3. c = #1674.

Explanation = Field (7a) concerns the shield number of the arresting officer. The arresting officer was Officer Roland, whose shield number was #1674.

4. a = Knife.

Explanation = Field (6) concerns the description of property vouchered. A Knife was vouchered by the officers.

Tips for Answering Police Forms Questions

- This question tests your comprehension skills. You need to be able to read a passage and pick out the key information;

- Remember to keep an eye out for important details such as voucher numbers and shield numbers. Additionally, make sure that the correct voucher, arrest, or shield number corresponds to the correct item, perpetrator, or officer;

- Carefully read the information in the text before even starting on the questions;

- Once you've started on the questions, re-read the passage to find the correct information.

Report-Structuring Questions

Question 1

b = 4, 2, 1, 3, 5.

Explanation = The report makes the most chronological and logical sense as follows:

I received a call from the dispatcher requesting a response to vandalism on 27th Street at 7:35pm. I arrived at the scene 5 minutes after receiving a signal from the dispatcher. I discovered a group of young men throwing rocks through a shop window. Most of the young men ran off when the police car arrived, although we were able to apprehend one of them. Myself and my partner took the individual into custody and returned them to the station, arriving at approximately 7:55pm.

Question 2

a = 2, 3, 4, 1, 5.

Explanation = The report makes the most chronological and logical sense as follows:

As I entered the room, the suspect immediately declared that they wanted a lawyer before proceeding. I advised the suspect of his rights after sitting down at the table in the interrogation room. I then asked the suspect where they were at 11:15pm the night before, where an individual who matches his description had been seen distributing illegal drugs. The suspect leaned back in their chair and refused to answer my question. I asked two more questions, but the suspect refused to answer either of them.

Question 3

d = 4, 5, 1, 3, 2.

Explanation = The report makes the most chronological and logical sense as follows:

While driving, I noticed a black SUV swerving in the road. I followed the SUV to see if the driver would continue to swerve or otherwise lose control of the vehicle. I signalled for the driver to pull over where it was safe for him to do so. I performed a breathalyzer test to confirm that he was over the legal alcohol limit for driving. I placed the driver under arrest and drove him to the station so that he could be processed.

Tips for Answering Report-Structuring Questions

*   This question type assesses your ability to examine a series of sentences and structure them in a way which makes the most sense;

*   Try to place the sentences in an order which makes the most sense when reading it. Once you've chosen an order, read it back to yourself to see if it sounds right in your head;

*   If you're allowed to, you might find it helpful to write out the sentences yourself and see how much sense they make. Seeing them grouped as a paragraph sometimes makes it easier to spot whether it makes sense or not;

*   Make sure that the sentences are also ordered in a way which makes chronological sense. For example, the officer needs to pull over the car before they perform a breathalyzer test on the driver.

Sketches Questions

1. a = Face 1.

Explanation = Faces 2 and 3 are clearly feminine faces, whilst Face 1 is identical to the suspect's face in every way apart from the hairstyle.

Tips for Answering Sketches Questions

- For this question type, you need to be able to carefully examine the first sketch, and then decide on whether it could be a match for other sketches;

- You need to consider facial features which **do** change and those which **do not** change. Hairstyle, facial hair, and even facial scars are all subject to change. However, features such as skin tone, eye color, and facial structure are less likely to change in a short space of time;

- For these questions, you are usually told to assume that the subject has not received any facial reconstructive surgery. Therefore, focus on matching the subject with other images which share a similar facial structure.

Wanted Poster Questions

1. b = Subject Two.

    Explanation = The details in the wanted poster tell us that the subject is travelling with her three-year-old son.

2. d = Subject Four.

    Explanation = The details in the wanted poster tell us that the subject uses card games when defrauding his victims.

3. a = Subject One.

    Explanation = The details in the wanted poster tell us that the subject spends his racketeering money at local strip clubs.

4. c = Subject Three.

    Explanation = The description of the subject on the wanted poster states that the subject has a tattoo of an anchor on his left bicep.

Tips for Answering Wanted Poster Questions

*   The key to this kind of question is to devote your attention both to the information below the image and the image itself. The questions asked will involve your knowledge of both, so you need to commit the entire wanted poster to memory;

*   Remember that this is a form of memory test, so you won't be able to look back at the wanted posters once you've started answering the questions. So, try to pair up the vital details on a wanted poster with the face of the subject;

*   Look out for unusual features which distinguish each subject, and try to mentally attach those to key information you might be asked about. For example, if one subject has a scar on his neck and is also known for using spiked knuckles during assaults, try to link this information in your head so it will be easier to answer the questions;

*   Like with other memory questions, don't spend too long staring blankly at the questions for this section. If you think that there's absolutely no chance of remembering what information matches the subject, then make an educated guess and move on to the next question.

Writing Reports Questions

Part 1

Question 1

d = All or none of the above are accurate.

Explanation = Each statement contains inaccuracies. They are:

a. The tense of the sentence changes from present tense (swerves) to past tense (drove). Either 'swerves' should be changed to 'swerved', or 'drove' should be changed to 'drives'.

b. This sentence spells 'too' incorrectly. The witness was 'too' tired to focus, not 'to' tired to focus.

c. This statement spells perpetrator incorrectly.

Question 2

b = The Officer spent a long time in the building.

Explanation = Statements a and c contain inaccuracies, whilst b is clear of inaccuracies:

a. This sentence should read "The arrest was made quickly", not "The arrest was made quick".

c. This sentence uses 'was' when it should be using 'were'. This is because 'people' is a plural.

Question 3

b = The dog had barked all morning.

Explanation = Statements a and c contain inaccuracies, whilst statement b is clear of inaccuracies:

a. In this sentence, 'there' should be replaced with 'their', since the tyres belong to a person in question.

c. This sentence uses 'where' instead of 'were'.

Part 2

Question 1

b = An Asian male, 20 years old, assaulted a 45-year-old black male at Micah's Barbers (42 107th Street) at 3:35pm. The suspect used both his fists and a metal baseball bat during the assault. The crime was reported by one of the barbers working at the barbershop.

Explanation = This is the most accurate report since the suspect was an Asian male of 20 years old, the victim was a 45-year-old black male, and the incident occurred at Micah's Barbers at 3:35pm. The time or reporting details that one of the barbers called the police.

Question 2

c = At approximately 11:30am, an unknown white male stole a car from the parking lot of the Peak Valley business park. The car belonged to a 33-year-old white male.

Explanation = The time of occurrence was 11:30am, and the suspect was an unknown white male. The report does not state whether the vehicle was broken into or not, only that it was stolen. The car indeed belonged to a 33-year-old white male.

Question 3

d = At 11:15pm, a 23-year-old white female was spotted vandalising Maude's Bar (23, 12th Street). The crime was reported at 11:20pm.

Explanation = The time of occurrence was 11:15pm. The suspect was a 23-year-old white female. The crime was vandalism, and the place of occurrence was Maude's Bar (23 12th Street). The crime was reported at 11:20pm.

Tips for Answering Writing Reports Questions

* The first type of question is simply testing your spelling, grammar, punctuation, and syntax skills;

* Learn common errors such as 'to', 'too', and 'two', and 'there', 'their', and 'they're'. These have a good chance of appearing in

this section;

- Take some time to create a list of words which you know that you struggle with. Then, find the correct spellings and take some time to memorize them;

- Remember that the majority of sentences and statements that you have to read and assess will be related to police work. Therefore, you shouldn't be too worried about anomalous words such as 'capillaries' appearing in your test;

- The second type of question is assessing your ability to carefully read information and decide on the answer option which best matches the text. Cross-reference the information in the answer option with the information in the report to ensure that your answer most accurately represents the data in the passage.

EXAM TIPS

Exams can be difficult, and you need to prepare for them in two different ways. First, you need to know the content of the exam. This is the actual information that you are going to be tested on – the stuff you've been learning in lessons.

Come Prepared

Always make sure that you have all of the equipment necessary for completing an exam. What you're allowed will depend on the specific department you're testing with, so make sure to check beforehand.

The following are things that you can take into almost any exam:

* **Black pens.** You should always take a few black ballpoint pens into your exams. You may not be allowed to use blue ink or other types of pens - ballpoints are the standard.

* **Bottle of water.** Bringing a bottle of water into an exam can help you concentrate – you don't want to get dehydrated. Check with your relevant department to see if they allow water in the exam.

Keep Calm

Getting a handle on your nerves can be really difficult during the run up to your exam, but remember that this is completely normal. If you consider that doing well in your exams is very important, then it would be bizarre for you not to be at least a bit nervous. Millions of people will be going through the same thing as you, and millions more have been in your position and have made it out of the other end in one piece. Life goes on after your exam, even if it doesn't feel like that during the heat of the moment.

Exams are stressful, and the conditions you take them in aren't pleasant either. Being stuck in a silent room for an hour, with nothing but a question paper and your own thoughts, can be incredibly daunting. However, you need to remember that you're not the only one who feels this way, and that a bit of nerves can give you the boost you need in the exam hall.

That said, you need to keep any anxiety under control. A breakdown just before the exam (or even worse, during it) is uncommon, but just remember that not doing as well as you'd hoped in a single exam isn't the end of the world.

You might feel as though you aren't prepared enough, or perhaps a peer has made you unsure about what you've revised – minutes before entering the exam room. This happens often, and be incredibly demoralising. Remember that how prepared you think you are doesn't necessarily represent how well prepared you actually are. Sometimes, people who feel poorly prepared for some exams in the minutes before taking it end up doing incredibly well, and some people find themselves doing worse in exams that they felt completely ready for. Essentially, you never truly know how prepared you are.

Besides, what's the use in worrying on the day of the exam? There's no time left to go back and revise some more, so there's no point in getting stressed about it once you're in the room. Try and get into the current moment and power through it.

Here are some other tips for keeping calm in the exam:

- **Breathing exercises.** If you find yourself getting nervous before exams, or struggle to get to sleep due to exam anxiety, then breathing exercises could be beneficial.

- **Get into the moment.** Just before and during your exam, it can help to go into "exam-mode". By this, we mean blocking off outside distractions and any negativity coming from anywhere. Sometimes, hearing people talk about the possible contents of the exam just before entering can put you off. It might make you feel as if you've missed out on something major, and then cause you to worry once you enter the exam room. Put all of this out of your mind as soon as you enter the room. Once you're in the exam, there's no use fretting about those details.

- **Positive thinking**. This might seem obvious, but thinking positively about the exam and what comes after can be extremely helpful. Some people like to change their mind-set about exams, thinking of it as an opportunity to show off their knowledge, rather than as a painful task that they have to work their way through. Alternatively, focus on what you **do** know rather than what you **don't** know, what you **can** do rather than what you **can't** do. Once you're in the exam room, there's no point worrying about your weaknesses. Focus on your strengths.

-

Read Instructions Carefully

This sounds simple, but far too many people trip up on this simple bit of advice. When you enter your exam, the first thing you should do is read the instructions on the front of the question or answer paper. In some cases, an invigilator may read the instructions to you, but feel free to read the instructions before the exam starts.

Keep an eye out for instructions on what questions to answer. In some exams, you'll have a choice of which questions you answer, rather than having to answer every question. In these cases, you need to make sure that you know exactly what's required of you, so that you don't waste time answering questions that you don't need to answer. The only thing worse than finding out at the end of the exam that you answered questions unnecessarily, is realising that you didn't answer enough of them!

When you are given a choice of two or more questions to answer (especially in essay subjects), make sure you clearly show which questions you are answering. In some exams, you'll have to tick a box to show what question you're attempting, whilst others will require you to write the question number in your answer section. Either way, keep an eye on the instructions before going ahead and starting the question. This will prevent you from wasting time answering questions that you don't need to attempt, and also stop you from accidentally missing questions that need answering.

Answer the Easiest Questions First

This tip is absolutely key for the tougher exams you come across, since it's an excellent way to use your time in the exam hall effectively.

Say you're about to sit an exam. You sit down and have the examination instructions read out to you. The invigilator instructs you to start your exam, and then you begin. You open the question booklet to find that the first question seems almost impossible. Before you panic, take a flick through the booklet and take a look at some of the other questions. If possible, pick the question that looks the easiest to you and start with that.

This is a good technique for two reasons. Firstly, it's a great boost to your confidence when you're feeling unsure about the exam. There's not much worse in an exam than sitting there, becoming more and more demoralised by a question that you don't think you can answer. Starting with more manageable questions will help you ease into the exam, and hopefully you'll recall some information while doing it.

Sometimes, exams can fit together like a puzzle. At first, it seems impossible. But, once you start to put pieces in (answer the questions), the more difficult bits start to make sense. All of a sudden, you're on a roll of answering questions, and then the tough ones don't seem so bad!

The other reason that this is a good technique, is that it represents a good use of your time. There's no point sitting and staring blankly at a question that you can't solve, when there are others that you could be getting on with. Forget about the tough questions for now, bank as many marks you can get with the easier ones, then go back to the hard ones at the end if you have time. This way, you can secure as many marks as possible. In the worst-case scenario, you won't be able to complete the tough questions, but you'll still have earned a few points for all of the others.

Double-Check Your Work

Everyone makes mistakes. It's almost completely unavoidable, even under relaxed conditions, to create a piece of work that's free of any errors at all. In an exam, you're going to feel a bit rushed, and you're probably going to be working very quickly. This is fine, but remember that you're more likely to make mistakes this way. So, it's important that you go back and check everything you've written. Small, silly errors can cost you big marks, so it's vital to make sure you've fixed anything that could be wrong.

Proofreading can take place at two times during your exam. You can either re-read each of your answers individually after you've completed each one, or you can go back at the end of the exam (if you have time) and check every question in one go. There are benefits and drawbacks to both:

Proofread as you go

Pros	Cons
You're more likely to have time to double-check your answers	If you spend too long proofreading, you might not finish the exam
You can take the exam bit by bit	You might be in "exam-mode" and not be as relaxed as at the end of the exam

Proofread at the end

Pros	Cons
You can focus on finishing the exam first before going back to check	If you take too long doing the exam, you might not have time to proofread towards the end
You'll probably be more relaxed once you've answered all the questions	

Both have pros and cons, and one method may just suit you better. You might prefer the methodical approach of checking every answer once you've finished it. Alternatively, you might find it easier to handle the exam, knowing that you've answered every question that you can, and then go back and check everything in one go.

Bring Some Water and Eat Healthily

You are allowed to bring a bottle of water into almost any exam. There may be a couple of exceptions for practical-based exams – such as Art, but aside from that, water is allowed. In fact, bringing a bottle of water to drink in an exam is largely encouraged, because it can help you relax and concentrate.

Some studies show that students who take a bottle of water into their exams and drink it get an average score of 5% higher than students who do not. While this might not actually happen for you, this suggests that having a bottle of water handy can be helpful.

On the same topic, eating healthily (and sensibly!) before your exams can make a big difference. Try and avoid drinking fizzy drinks or eating sweets before an exam. The sugar rush might make you feel on top of the world when the exam starts, but you could have a crash halfway through, leaving you shattered for the final stretch. Instead, try and have a good breakfast in the morning before your exams. See what works best for you, but eggs and fish (such as smoked salmon) can give you plenty of energy to complete your exams with.

In addition to this, some exams may allow you to bring in a small piece of food to eat. Fruit is always a safe bet, including bananas and apples. Basically, you want something that doesn't take too long to eat, but gives you enough of a boost to help you through the exam. Remember to check that you're allowed to take food into your exam before doing so.

Stay Healthy

No matter what happens in your exams, it's important that you stay healthy. This is a slightly more general point, but it can't be emphasised enough.

First, you need to stay mentally healthy. Remember that there's life after your exams, and so you shouldn't put yourself under unnecessary pressure. Some anxiety is unavoidable, but it's important that you don't let it get out of control. Between exams, remember to do things that you enjoy, be it sports, video-games, reading fiction, watching television or spending time with friends or family. This will help you to feel calm during your exam period, and remind you that there's more to life than your exams.

Secondly, you need to think about your physical wellbeing. While you're busy revising and making yourself ready to ace the exams, it's easy to forget about your own health. While it's good to take revision seriously, you can't neglect your own physical needs, and so you should make sure to get a lot of the following during your exam period:

- **Sleep.** Everyone needs sleep in order to function, and you're no different! Teenagers and adults need between 8 and 10 hours of sleep per night, so you should be aiming for this as well. A good night's sleep, particularly the night before your exam, can make a world of difference on the day of the test. It will also help you massively during your revision time.

- **A balanced diet.** This can be easily overlooked, but being fed well can be the key to acing an exam on the day. You want to feel as prepared as possible, so be sure to get a good meal the night before and on the day of your exam. Also, try to eat plenty of fruit and vegetables, since they help strengthen your immune system. Some students work themselves extremely hard, then forget to boost their immunity, leading to colds and flu. You want to avoid this – being ill during an exam is horrible!

Planning and Timing Your Exam

Good planning and timing are two of the most important skills that you can learn and practise before sitting your exams. In fact, being able to plan effectively and get your timing down will serve you well in almost every career, so it pays to put the effort in now.

Before you go into your exam, you should find out exactly what the structure of the exam will be.

Try and find out the answers to the following questions:

• How long do I have for the whole exam?

• What type of questions will be asked (essay, single-word answer, short paragraph, problem solving, mathematical sums)?

• How many marks are there in the whole exam?

• Roughly, how many marks are available per question?

• If applicable, how much time is there for planning?

Once you have this information, you can get to work on applying this to your revision schedule. For example, when you attempt a mock exam, you should try to make the situation as close to the real thing as possible. You should plan and time your mock exam as if it were an actual exam.

POLICE OFFICER
MOCK TESTS

Explanation for the Mock Tests

In this chapter, we have supplied you with a range of practice test questions, all of which are based on the material which you learned in the sample questions chapter of this guide.

These practice questions have been divided into two separate tests. We advise that you complete one of the tests, then read the answers, before moving on to the second section. This is because you will get the opportunity to take a test, then check your results against our answers and explanations. From there, you can go back to the mock questions, do a little more practice, and then head into the second mock tests. This will put you in the best position for the real test.

Bear in mind that these mock tests will not necessarily match the content in your actual police officer entrance exam. The exam you take will differ depending on where and when you sit it. So, rather than trying to futilely cover every possible type of test you could sit, we've collected some of the most popular types of question and placed them in a mock test format. These tests are made of the same questions that we have used in the sample questions chapter. Therefore, you can make use of those sample questions to prepare yourself before taking our mock tests.

Make sure that you carefully read the information for each question before proceeding. Unlike the questions in the sample questions chapter, the types of question you'll be facing in the mock tests will not be clearly denoted. So, it will be up to you to figure out from the information and the questions themselves what it is that you need to do. This way, you'll be more prepared to quickly identify different question types in the real exam, and then be more likely to complete them in a way which is most likely to help you pass.

Each of the mock tests has ten sections, and most sections have either three or four questions. This means that, in total, you will have to answer between thirty and forty questions in each test. The time limit for each test is 45 minutes, meaning that you have between a minute and a minute and a half for each question.

Remember that your real test might be much longer, and it might even be shorter. However, this test should give you the opportunity to see how well you can answer the questions that you've prepared for within a specific time constraint.

Finally, we do recommend that you complete this test under the timed conditions that we've suggested. This way, you'll be able to see how well you work under pressure, and get as close to the real test as possible.

Good luck!

MOCK TEST 1

Section One

For the following question, read the passage in relation to the blank arrest report. Then, answer the four questions on the following pages.

On Tuesday 8th November 2016, at 23:56, police were called to the scene of a shooting in a bar in Ficshire. The bar was named Freesies, and was located in the south of Ficshire.

The officers attending the scene were Officer Paul Preston (shield #1137), Officer Wendy Smith (shield #3562) and Officer Bradley Nevis (shield #2365). When they arrived at the scene, they found a male victim dead on the pavement. Officer Wendy Smith quickly apprehended and arrested two suspects, one black female – Anita Gibbons, who was 34 years old, and one white male – Derek Matthews, who was 35 years old. Both Anita (arrest #6324) and Derek (arrest #6235) were taken to the police station for further questioning. Later, Derek was charged with 1 count of murder.

The victim was later identified as 21-year-old Gavin Brown. He had been shot once at close range in the temple, and had died instantly. The gun used was a black revolver. Upon further inspection of the two suspects, Derek Matthews was found to be carrying weapons ammunition. This ammunition was later matched to the bullet fired into Gavin Brown. Further investigation of the crime scene was conducted by Detective Wallace Morgan (shield #7423).

Arrest Report

Person(s) Arrested

(1a) Name:

(1b) Charge:

(1c) Description of Arrestee:

(1d) Arrest Number:

(2a) Name:

(2b) Charge:

(2c) Description of Arrestee:

(2d) Arrest Number:

(3) Time and Date of Occurrence (24-hour clock):

(3a) Place of Occurrence:

(4) Details of Offense:

(5) Place of Arrest:

(6) Time and Date of Arrest (24-hour clock):

(7) Description of Property Vouchered:

(7a) Voucher Number:

(8) Name of Arresting Officer:

(8a) Shield Number:

(9) Assignment of Arresting Officer:

(10) Detective Assigned for Follow-Up Investigation (name, shield number, assignment):

1. Which of the following should be entered into field (3a)?

   a. Freesies bar, North Ficshire.

   b. Freemons bar, South Ficshire.

   c. Freesies bar, South Ficshire.

   d. Freesies club, East Ficshire.

2. Which of the following should be entered into field (8a)?

   a. Shield #3562.

   b. Shield #2365.

   c. Shield #1137.

   d. Shield #6324.

3. Which of the following should be entered into field (2b)?

   a. Aggravated assault.

   b. Burglary.

   c. Breaking and entering.

   d. Murder.

4. Which of the following should be entered into field (1c)?

   a. Black female, 31 years old.

   b. Black female, 34 years old.

   c. White male, 36 years old.

   d. White male, 21 years old.

Section Two

For the following questions, you will be given an extended passage to read. You have ten minutes to read the passage, and commit as much information to memory as possible. Your goal is to focus on the most important information, such as names, dates, times, and other details about the crime. Once you have spent ten minutes reading the text, turn the page and begin to answer the questions based on the information you can recall about the passage. Once you have turned over, you cannot return to re-read the passage.

At 12:32pm, on the afternoon of Thursday, March 15, 2018, police officers were called to a scene on Bakers Street. The call had been placed by a man named Henri Hummer. Mr Hummer reported that there were three youths in his shop, who were subjecting him to racial abuse.

When the police arrived at the scene, they found that the youths were still in Mr Hummer's shop, subjecting him to taunts and abuse. One of the youths, known only as 'Fingers', was taking objects from the shelves and tossing them at Mr Hummer. This include a packet of potato chips, candy bars, and a can of soda.

Immediately, the police officers intervened. Officer Dibble restrained 'Fingers', pinning him to the floor. Although the young man put up quite a fight, Officer Dibble was able to place handcuffs over his wrists. In response, one of the other youths leapt over the counter, and grabbed Mr Hummer. The youth pulled out a black, customised handgun, and put it to the shopkeeper's head. He demanded that the police release 'Fingers' immediately. Grudgingly, Officer Dibble and his co-worker – Officer Harris – agreed.

As soon as the handcuffs were removed from 'Fingers', he jumped up, and aimed a profanity at the police. He then ran out of the store, closely followed by his two associates. On the way out of the store, one of his associates dropped an ID card. Upon closer inspection, Officer Harris observed that the photo on the card did not match the physical characteristics of any of the suspects. The card belonged to a man named Jeff.

5. Which of the officers placed handcuffs on 'Fingers'?

   a. Officer Dibble.

   b. Officer Smith.

   c. Officer Harris.

   d. Officer Brimley.

6. What was the colour of the handgun that 'Fingers' used?

   a. Black.

   b. Silver.

   c. Green.

   d. None of these.

7. How many youths were at the scene?

   a. 1.

   b. 2.

   c. 3.

   d. 4.

8. Which of the following was thrown at Mr Hummer?

   a. Potato chips and candy bars.

   b. Bottles of alcohol.

   c. Potato chips.

   d. Candy bars.

Section Three

Read the following passage carefully, then answer the proceeding four questions on the following pages, based solely on the information in the passage.

On Tuesday 26th August, 2015, police were called to attend the scene of a crime. The incident had taken place at a local shopping mall, in the town of Ficshire. When police arrived at the scene, they were informed that the shopping centre security team had apprehended two youths. The two youths were caught shoplifting from a clothing store. The clothing store was named Missy's, and sold items for girls aged 10-15. The logo of Missy's is a handbag. The suspects had stolen a lipstick container, two pairs of shoes, and a green dress.

Officer Edwards, and her colleague Officer Sterling, went downstairs to meet the security team. They entered a room, passing through a green door, where the two suspects were sitting at a desk – being guarded by a security officer named Morgan. Morgan informed Officer Edwards that the two suspects were known for causing trouble at the shopping centre. Although they were just 13 and 14 years of age, Morgan recommended that they were jailed for a very long time.

Officer Edwards informed Morgan that she would be happy to take care of this incident from here on out, and would escort the two individuals to the police station. Unfortunately, Morgan was not happy with this solution. He refused to allow the two suspects to leave without a guarantee that they would be sent to jail. When Officer Sterling informed him that this was something that would be dealt with externally, Morgan became aggressive and tried to physically accost her. As a result, Officer Edwards was forced to place him under arrest.

9. How old were the two shoplifters in this incident?

  a. 13 and 15 years old.

  b. 10 and 15 years old.

  c. 13 and 14 years old.

  d. 12 and 13 years old.

10. Which of the following is true about the incident that took place?

  a. The two suspects were released by the police with no further charges.

  b. The security team did not allow the police to see the suspects.

  c. In order to enter the security room, Officers Edwards and Sterling needed to pass through a red door.

  d. The two suspects were known to the shopping centre security team, before this incident took place.

11. The store that the two youths stole from has which of the following as its logo?

  a. A handbag.

  b. A pair of shoes.

  c. A crocodile.

  d. A lipstick container.

12. Which of the following was stolen from the store?

  a. A red dress.

  b. A tiara.

  c. Eyeliner and lipstick.

  d. None of the above.

Section Four

Read the following passages, and then choose the correct answer based on the information in the text, as well as what is most likely to be true.

13. A homicide occurred in an apartment block on 75th Street in the 19th Precinct. Four witnesses gave descriptions of the perpetrator, all of which differ. Which of the following descriptions is most likely to be correct?

   a. Male, white, 20 years old, 5'2", bald, white t-shirt, brown eyes.

   b. Male, white, 20 years old, 5'9", bald, white t-shirt, brown eyes.

   c. Male, white, 30 years old, 5'9", brown hair, white t-shirt, blue eyes.

   d. Male, white, 25 years old, 5'9", brown hair, black suit, brown eyes.

14. Four witnesses gave their account of a suspect in a hit and run incident. Which of the following descriptions is most likely to be correct?

   a. Red sportscar, smashed windshield.

   b. Black SUV, dent in rear left-passenger door.

   c. Black sedan.

   d. White sedan.

15. Four witnesses gave their account of the goods a suspect left with during a robbery of a jewelry store. Which of the following descriptions is most likely to be correct?

a. Laptop.

b. Necklace.

c. Vase.

d. Ornate pen.

16. Four witnesses gave their account of the weapon used in an assault on Main Street last night at 8:45pm. Which of the following descriptions is most likely to be correct?

a. Katana.

b. Switchblade.

c. Brass knuckles.

d. Hatchet.

Section Five

The following questions measure your arithmetic skills. You must answer the following arithmetic questions without the aid of a calculator.

A significant case of insurance fraud perpetrated by individuals in the 26th Precinct led to large amount of money being fraudulently acquired. The list of individual occurrences is as follows:

> 1 destroyed sportscar = $60,000 total.
>
> 1 burnt-down house = $275,000 total.
>
> 4 stolen laptops = $10,000 total.

17. What was the total amount of money defrauded during this case?

a. $335,000.

b. $355,000.

c. $350,000.

d. $345,000.

18. How much was each stolen laptop worth?

a. $2,000.

b. $2,500.

c. $3,000.

d. $1,500.

19. What's the total amount that was fraudulently acquired, minus the destroyed sportscar?

a. $265,000.

b. $280,000.

c. $385,000.

d. $285,000.

Section Six

For the following question, you will be given a sketch of an area to examine. You have five minutes to study the image, and commit as much information to memory as possible. You should try to focus on any information that might be important, such as license plates on vehicles, names of places, and other details which might seem important.

20. What is the name of the building to the left of the hotel?

   a. Police Station.

   b. Inn.

   c. School.

   d. Department Store.

21. How many people are crossing the road?

   a. 4.

   b. 3.

   c. 2.

   d. 5.

22. How many children are playing in the park?

   a. 4.

   b. 2.

   c. 3.

   d. 5.

23. There is a man standing by a lamp-post outside of the school. What is he holding in his hand?

   a. Baseball bat.

   b. Briefcase.

   c. Guitar.

   d. Backpack.

Section Seven

For these questions, read the information in each passage. Then choose the most logical order for the information to appear in if you were writing a report.

Officer Daniels is writing a report concerning arson. His report consists of the following five sentences:

1. The flames were starting to rise, and smoke was filling the air. I then noticed several youths standing by the corner, holding a can of gasoline. They appeared to be laughing and making jokes about the fire.

2. I immediately called the fire department, whilst my partner detained the youths.

3. My partner and I arrived at the scene within 10 minutes. We immediately noticed that one of the buildings, a bookshop, was on fire.

4. Three of the youths were later charged with criminal damage.

5. At 4:33pm, I received a call from a member of the public, informing me that a group of youths were playing with a tank of gasoline on Freamon Avenue.

24. Which order of the above sentences makes the most logical sense?

  a. 5, 1, 3, 2, 4.

  b. 5, 3, 1, 2, 4.

  c. 5, 2, 1, 3, 4.

  d. 4, 5, 1, 3, 2.

Section Eight

For the following question type, you need to closely read and examine the four wanted posters over the next four pages. This is a form of memory test, so you will need to memorize the details of the images as well as the information beneath them. You have five minutes to read and examine all four of the wanted posters.

Once five minutes have passed, turn over and answer the questions based purely on the information that you have remembered from the wanted posters. You need to match the correct subject's image to the details in each question.

Subject 1

WANTED FOR GRAND LARCENY

Michael 'Mike' Johnson

Age: 45.

Race: White.

Height: 5'10".

Weight: 160 pounds.

Sex: Male.

Eye Color: Green.

Hair: Gray

Tattoo(s): None.

Scars: Curved scar on neck.

Subject poses as a depot worker, making his way into depots and stealing products which were due to be shipped. Recently suspected of stealing over $20000 worth of fashion products. Previously served in prison for assault.

Subject 2

WANTED FOR PROSTITUTION

Rebecca Erikson

Age: 23

Race: White.

Height: 5'4"

Weight: 125 pounds.

Sex: Female.

Eye Color: Blue.

Hair: Blonde.

Tattoo(s): Barbed wire around left-shoulder.

Scars: None.

Subject has been grooming younger women to be work for her as prostitutes, whilst also working as a prostitute herself.

Subject 3

WANTED FOR GRAND LARCENY

Lupé Alvarez	
Age: 41	Eye Color: Brown.
Race: Hispanic.	Hair: Brown.
Height: 5'6".	Tattoo(s): None.
Weight: 145 pounds.	Scars: Three scars above right eyebrow.
Sex: Female.	

Subject shot and killed another woman after a minor traffic collision escalated into violence. The subject has been previously arrested for assault, and suffers from alcoholism.

Subject 4

WANTED FOR MURDER

Daniel 'Danny' McCabe.

Age: 36

Eye Color: Brown.

Race: White.

Hair: Brown.

Height: 6'0".

Tattoo(s): Skull on upper back.

Weight: 165 pounds.

Scars: None.

Sex: Male.

Subject wanted for assaulting victim with a pool cue at a bar on 25th Street. Subject is known for spending time on the street, shouting conspiracy theories at anyone who passes him.

25. Which of the subjects is known for shouting about conspiracy theories?

   a. Subject One.

   b. Subject Two.

   c. Subject Three.

   d. Subject Four.

26. Which of the subjects has a tattoo of a skull on their upper back?

   a. Subject One.

   b. Subject Two.

   c. Subject Three.

   d. Subject Four.

27. Which of the subjects has been grooming young women to work as prostitutes?

   a. Subject One.

   b. Subject Two.

   c. Subject Three.

   d. Subject Four.

28. Which of the subjects poses as a depot worker?

   a. Subject One.

   b. Subject Two.

   c. Subject Three.

   d. Subject Four.

Section Nine

For the following questions, you need to use your understanding of probability to find the correct answers. You might also need to use some outside knowledge to find the correct answer.

Read the following passages, and then choose the correct answer based on the information in the text, as well as what is most likely to be true.

29. A robbery took place at an apartment building in the 12th Precinct. There were four witnesses present, each of which gave a different description of the perpetrator. Which of the following descriptions is most likely to be correct?

    a. Female, white, 30 years old, 5'4", white vest and blue jeans.

    b. Female, white, 60 years old, 5'10", white vest and blue jeans.

    c. Female, white, 30 years old, 5'10", white vest and blue jeans.

    d. Female, white, 30 years old, 6'2", black suit.

30. An assault occurred outside a church on Lincoln Avenue. The victim was severely beaten. There were four witnesses present, each of which gave a different description of the weapon used in the assault. Which of the following descriptions is most likely to be correct?

    a. Spiked Mace.

    b. Handgun.

    c. Baseball bat.

    d. Guitar.

31. A drive-by shooting occurred in the 19th Precinct. Three shooters were seen. There were four witnesses present, each of which gave a different description of the vehicle used in the shooting. Which of the following descriptions is most likely to be correct?

    a. Motorbike.

    b. Sedan.

c. SUV.

d. Sportscar.

32. A mugging occurred in the 45th Precinct. Four witnesses were present, each of which gave a different description of the suspect. Which of the following descriptions is most likely to be correct?

e. White, male, 5'4", white t-shirt and blue jeans, green eyes.

f. White, male, 5'9", white t-shirt and blue jeans, green eyes.

g. White, male, 6'2", white t-shirt and blue jeans, brown eyes.

h. White, male, 5'9", white t-shirt and blue jeans, brown eyes.

Section Ten

For each of the following questions, you will be given a series of three statements. Your task is to read each statement and decide on whether or not they are grammatically accurate, clearly-written, and free from spelling errors. Choose the statement which is the most accurate and well-written (i.e. the one which has no grammar or spelling errors). If you believe that none or all of the statements have these errors, then choose option D.

33. Evaluate the following statements:

   a. The drunk driver was drived through the town.

   b. The woman claimed that she had no recollection of the events.

   c. The man jumped out of the window to escapes.

   d. All or none of the above are accurate.

34. Evaluate the following statements:

   a. Officer Daniels found no evidence to suggest murder.

   b. There was substantial evidence of drug usage.

   c. The police had conducted an illegal wiretap.

   d. All or none of the above are accurate.

35. Evaluate the following statements:

   a. The man was drunk, and crashed his carz.

   b. The dog, had, been wandering the street?

   c. Officer Daniels had made a breakthrough in the case.

   d. All or none of the above are accurate.

Answers to Mock Test 1

Section One

1 .c = Freesies bar, South Ficshire.

Explanation = The first paragraph states the following:

"The bar was named Freesies, and was located in the south of Ficshire."

2. a = Shield #3562.

Explanation = Field (8a) is concerned with the Shield Number of the arresting officer. The arresting officer was Wendy Smith, whose Shield Number is #3562.

3. d = Murder.

Explanation = Field (2b) is concerned with the crime which the suspect is being charged for. The second paragraph states that Derek was charged with one count of murder. Since he was the second person to be arrested, his details appear in field (2a), (2b), (2c), and so on. Therefore, 'murder' should be entered into field (2b).

4. b = Black female, 34 years old.

Explanation = Field (1c) is concerned with the description of the first arrestee. The description of the first arrestee reads:

"one black female – Anita Gibbons, who was 34 years old,"

Therefore, the information to be entered into field (1c) is "black female, 34 years old".

Section Two

5. a = Officer Dibble.

Explanation = The third paragraph states:

"Although the young man put up quite a fight, Officer Dibble was able to place handcuffs over his wrists."

6. d = None of these.

Explanation = Fingers was not the youth wielding a firearm. Therefore, no color is correct.

7. c = 3.

Explanation = The first paragraph states:

"Mr Hummer reported that there were three youths in his shop"

8. a = Potato chips and candy bars.

Explanation = The second paragraph states:

"One of the youths, known only as 'Fingers', was taking objects from the shelves and tossing them at Mr Hummer. This included a packet of potato chips, candy bars, and a can of soda."

Section Three

9. c = 13 and 14 years old.

Explanation = The second paragraph states:

"Although they were just 13 and 14 years of age, Morgan recommended that they were jailed for a very long time."

10. d = The two suspects were known to the shopping mall security team, before this incident took place.

Explanation = The second paragraph states:

"Morgan informed Officer Edwards that the two suspects were known for causing trouble at the shopping centre."

Therefore, the two suspects were known to the shopping mall security team before the incident took place.

11. a = A handbag.

Explanation = The first paragraph states:

"The two youths were caught shoplifting from a clothing store. The clothing store was named Missy's, and sold items for girls aged 10-15. The logo of Missy's is a handbag."

The girls shoplifted from Missy's. Missy's logo is a handbag. Therefore, the store the girls shoplifted from has a logo of a handbag.

12. d = None of the above.

Explanation = The first paragraph states:

"The suspects had stolen a lipstick container, two pairs of shoes, and a green dress."

Therefore, the two girls did not shoplift a red dress, tiara, or eyeliner and lipstick.

Section Four

13. b = Male, white, 20 years old, 5'9", bald, white t-shirt, brown eyes.

Explanation = Brown eyes are more common than blue eyes, which makes answer option B more likely than C. White t-shirts are more common than suits, making option B more likely than C. 5'9" is a more common height for males than 5'2", making option B more likely than option C. Therefore, option B is the most likely to be true.

14. c = Black sedan.

Explanation = Black sedans are more common than white sedans, black SUVs, and red sportscars.

15. b = Necklace.

Explanation = The store being stolen from is a jewelry store. Generally speaking, there are going to be more necklaces in a jewelry store than laptops, vases, and ornate pens. Therefore, a necklace is the most likely thing to be stolen from a jewelry store.

16. b = Switchblade.

Explanation = Switchblades are more common than katanas, brass knuckles, and hatchets.

Section Five

17. d = $345,000.

Explanation = This is the sum of all the occurrences. 1 destroyed sportscar ($60,000), 1 burnt-down house ($275,000), and 4 stolen laptops ($10,000 total).

$60,000 + $275,000 + $10,000 = $345,000.

18. b = $2,500.

Explanation = Four laptops were stolen, and the total value of the four stolen laptops is $10,000. Therefore, we need to divide $10,000 by four to find the value of each laptop.

$10,000 ÷ 4 = $2,500.

19. d = $285,000.

Explanation = To get this answer, we need to add the total of the items, apart from the sportscar.

$275,000 + $10,000 = $285,000.

Section Six

20. b = Inn.

Explanation = The name above the building to the left of the hotel reads 'Inn'.

21. c = 2.

Explanation = The bottom-left crossing shows two people currently crossing the road.

22. d = 5.

Explanation = There are five children in the park. One is on the swing, the other is to the right of the swing, one is to the left of the swing, one is to the left of the right-most tree, and one is further left of the right-most tree.

23. b = Briefcase.

Explanation = The man standing by the lamppost near to car next to the school is holding a briefcase in his hand.

Section Seven

24. b = 5, 3, 1, 2, 4.

Explanation = This order reads as the following:

At 4:33pm, I received a call from a member of the public, informing me that a group of youths were playing with a tank of gasoline on Freamon Avenue. My partner and I arrived at the scene within 10 minutes. We immediately noticed that one of the buildings, a bookshop, was on fire. The flames were starting to rise, and smoke was filling the air. I then noticed several youths standing by the corner, holding a can of gasoline. They appeared to be laughing and making jokes about the fire. I immediately called the fire department, whilst my partner detained the youths. Three of the youths were later charged with criminal damage.

Section Eight

25. d = Subject Four.

Explanation = It is stated on Subject Four's wanted poster that they are known for indulging in conspiracy theories and shouting about them in the street.

26. d = Subject Four.

Explanation = The subject description for Subject Four states that the subject has a tattoo of a skull on their upper back.

27. b = Subject Two.

Explanation = It is stated on Subject Two's wanted poster that they have been grooming young women to work as prostitutes.

28. a = Subject One.

Explanation = It is stated on Subject One's wanted poster that they pose as a depot worker in order to infiltrate depots and steal goods.

Section Nine

29. a = Female, white, 30 years old, 5'4", white vest and blue jeans.

Explanation = The average height of women in the USA is 5'4". Therefore, answer option A is most likely to be correct.

30. c = Baseball bat.

Explanation = The question states that the victim was severely beaten. This means that it was unlikely that a handgun was used in the assault. Apart from the handgun, the most common weapon is the baseball bat. Therefore, the baseball bat is the description which is most likely correct.

31. b = Sedan.

Explanation = Three shooters were spotted, which means that it was unlikely that a motorbike was used in the shooting. From the rest of these options, sedans are the most common. Therefore, the sedan is most likely to be the correct description.

32. d = White, male, 5'9", white t-shirt and blue jeans, brown eyes.

Explanation = The height of 5'9" is the average for males in the USA. Likewise, brown eyes are more common than green eyes. Therefore, the description in answer option D is most likely to be correct.

Section Ten

33. b = The woman claimed that she had no recollection of the events.

Explanation = Answer option A is an inaccurate statement because 'drived' is not a word. The word which should be used is 'driven'. Answer option C misspells 'escape'. Answer option B has no inaccuracies in it.

34. d = All or none of the above are accurate.

Explanation = Each of the three sentences is free from any grammatical, spelling, and syntactical errors.

35. c = Officer Daniels had made a breakthrough in the case.

Explanation = Answer option A spells 'car' incorrectly. Answer option B incorrectly uses a question mark. Answer option C is completely free from grammatical, syntactical, and spelling errors.

MOCK TEST 2

Section One

Read the following passage carefully, then answer the proceeding four questions on the following pages, based solely on the information in the passage.

On the 24th May 2017, police arrived at Ficshire hospital, where they were to interview a young man. The man was named Kevin, and he had been savagely beaten whilst on his way home from work. The attack took place on Tuesday. It was now Thursday, and the officers had some serious questions to ask Kevin.

When they arrived at the hospital, the officers were directed to Room 2, on the first floor. They entered Kevin's room. Kevin was laying on the bed. His face was barely distinguishable from the wounds, and he could only communicate with officers via a speech synthesiser – which read out words as he typed them.

Kevin initially seemed very reluctant to speak to the officers. He informed them that he had been attacked for 'snitching', and that he had learned a valuable lesson about opening his mouth. Upon further persuasion by Officer Trueman, Kevin admitted that he also owed money to a well-known drug dealer in the area. He did not seem to believe that this was the reason for the attack. However, Officer Trueman later informed his partner that this was the most likely reason for the beating. Kevin left hospital the following Sunday.

On the Monday evening, Officer Trueman received a phone call. The call was from Inspector Harris, who informed Trueman that Kevin had been found dead. His body was found in a boarded-up house, in South Ficshire. Next to the body was a note that read, 'Snitch.'

1. Officer Trueman initially suspected that the attack was down to which of the following:

   a. Kevin informing on someone.

   b. Kevin owing money to someone.

   c. Kevin insulting someone behind their back.

   d. None of the above.

2. Which of the following statements is true?

a. The passage strongly implies that Kevin was attacked for 'snitching'.

b. The passage indicates that Officer Trueman did not believe that Kevin was telling the truth.

c. The passage strongly implies that Kevin was murdered by those whom he 'snitched on'.

d. The passage infers that Kevin's death was an act of suicide.

3. On what day of the week did the police visit Kevin at the hospital?

a. Monday.

b. Tuesday.

c. Thursday.

d. Saturday.

4. Which of the following is most accurate?

a. Kevin was shot by the drug dealer to whom he owed money.

b. Kevin was beaten up by the drug dealer to whom he owed money.

c. It is impossible to determine who attacked Kevin, based on the information given by the passage.

d. It is impossible for the police to determine who killed Kevin, based on the information given by the passage.

Section Two

For the following question, read the passage in relation to the blank arrest report. Then, answer the four questions on the following pages.

On Thursday 31st April, 2014, officers Weston (shield #6432) and Carrell (shield #2465) pulled over a black sedan, coming off the Ficshire highway, heading westbound. After asking the occupants of the sedan to step out of the vehicle, officer Carrell conducted a routine search of the interior, whilst Weston spoke to the owners.

Whilst searching the vehicle, Officer Carrell located an unlocked briefcase, which was found to be packed full of various narcotics. Immediately, Officer Weston arrested the occupants of the Sedan on drug possession charges. There were three occupants in total: Michael Martinez – a 24 year old Hispanic male (arrest #6823), Micha Kelly – a 22 year old white female (arrest #4235), and Javi Boatas – a 25 year old Hispanic male (arrest #1256).

Whilst being transported to the nearest police vehicle, Micha Kelly began to struggle with Officer Weston. As a result, the officers were forced to restrain her.

Further investigation of the car by Detective Bishop (shield #6362), a member of the narcotics investigation team, determined that the three arrested individuals were part of a major conspiracy to supply drugs across the town of Ficshire.

Arrest Report

Person(s) Arrested

(1a) Name:

(1b) Charge:

(1c) Description of Arrestee:

(1d) Arrest Number:

(2a) Name:

(2b) Charge:

(2c) Description of Arrestee:

(2d) Arrest Number:

(3) Time and Date of Occurrence (24-hour clock):

(3a) Place of Occurrence:

(4) Details of Offense:

(5) Place of Arrest:

(6) Time and Date of Arrest (24-hour clock):

(7) Description of Property Vouchered:

(7a) Voucher Number:

(8) Name of Arresting Officer:

(8a) Shield Number:

(9) Assignment of Arresting Officer:

(10) Detective Assigned for Follow-Up Investigation (name, shield number, assignment):

5. Which of the following should be entered into field (10)?

    a. Detective Bishop, shield #6362, narcotics investigation team.

    b. Detective Freamont, shield #8671, narcotics investigation team.

    c. Detective Bishop, shield #6362, narcotics investigation team.

    d. Detective Walker, shield #7143, narcotics investigation team.

6. Which of the following should be entered into field 8:

    a. Officer Weston.

    b. Officer Moore.

    c. Officer Nickels.

    d. Officer Broadshore.

7. Which of the following should be entered into field 1a:

    a. Michael Martinez.

    b. Michelle Martinez.

    c. Aaron Jackson.

    d. Wendy Smith.

8. Which of the following should be entered into field 8a:

    a. Shield #6432.

    b. Shield #4532.

    c. Shield #6423.

    d. Shield #6243.

Section Three

Read the following passage carefully, then answer the proceeding four questions on the following pages, based solely on the information in the passage.

On the morning of 5th November 2016, two officers were called to the scene of a car accident, in East Ficshire.

When they arrived at the scene, they discovered three vehicles. One vehicle, a red van, was laying on its side. The occupant of the vehicle, a woman with blonde hair, was sitting by the vehicle. The two other vehicles involved in the crash were a black sedan and a yellow convertible. The occupants of these two vehicles were rowing furiously. Nobody appeared to have sustained any injuries from this accident.

One of the officers went and spoke to the owner of the van, whilst the other officer – Sergeant Pearson – spoke to the other two drivers. Sergeant Pearson asked the two drivers to calm down. In response, the owner of the Sedan told Sergeant Pearson to mind his own business, and insulted him using a profanity. The owner of the sedan then got back into his vehicle, and drove away. Following this, the owner of the convertible apologised to Sergeant Pearson, and promised that she would fully cooperate with the police in any investigation that needed to be made.

The woman who owned the van then approached Sergeant Pearson. She informed him that she would be pressing charges against his colleague, for police brutality.

9. The owner of which of the following cars, agreed to comply fully with the police?

    a. Sedan.

    b. Van.

    c. Convertible.

    d. None of these.

10. What was the colour of the car that drove away from the scene?

a. Blue.

b. Silver.

c. Purple.

d. Black.

11. The owner of the sedan was...

a. Male.

b. Female.

c. Injured.

d. Drunk.

12. The owner of the van did which of the following?

a. Caused the accident to happen.

b. Accused Sergeant Pearson of police brutality.

c. Attacked the driver of the sedan.

d. Spoke to Sergeant Pearson's colleague.

Section Four

For the following question, you will be given a sketch of an area to examine. You have five minutes to study the image, and commit as much information to memory as possible. You should try to focus on any information that might be important, such as license plates on vehicles, names of places, and other details which might seem important.

Once this five-minute period has elapsed, turn over to the following page and answer the questions based on what you can remember about the image. At this point, you cannot look back at the image.

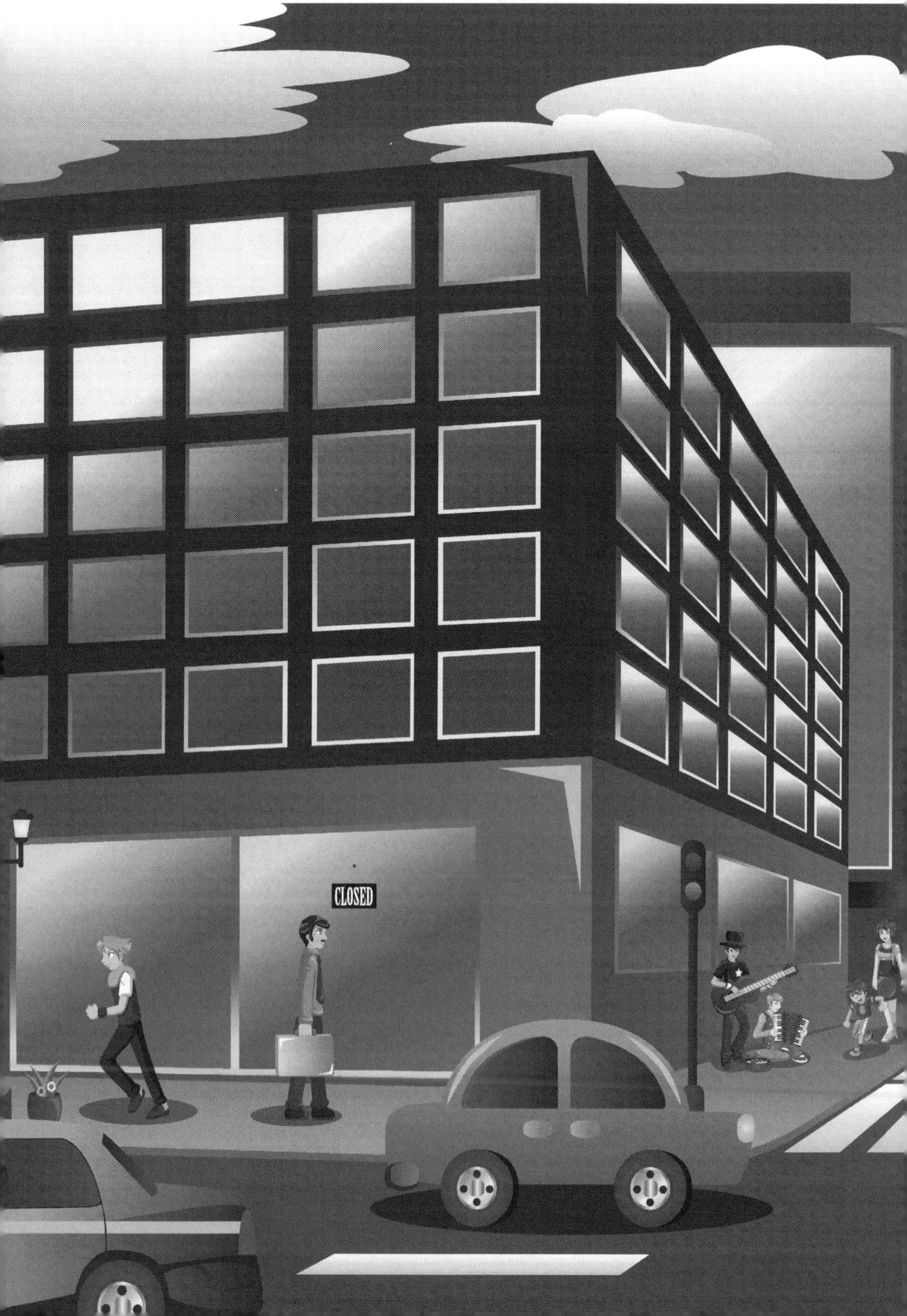
CLOSED

13. How many cars are on the road?

a. 4.

b. 3.

c. 2.

d. 5.

14. Which side of the road was the traffic light on?

a. Right-hand side.

b. Left-hand side.

c. Neither sides.

d. Both sides.

15. What's the name of the building on the right-hand side of the road?

a. Hotel.

b. Café.

c. Bar.

d. Liquor Store.

16. How many people are playing musical instruments in this image?

a. 3.

b. 4.

c. 1.

d. 2.

Section Five

For this section, read the information in each paragraph. Then, answer the three questions based purely on the information in the paragraph.

The Ficshire Police force are reviewing city-wide statistics from the past 6 months, as part of their bi-annual improvement process. In the past 6 months, drug related murders seem to have risen sharply. Specifically, in the north of Ficshire, there is an alarming trend of murders happening between the times when shift change over occurs, between 10 and 11pm. Between 10 and 11pm there are limited officers patrolling North Ficshire.

Although the body count in North Ficshire has increased, burglaries have dropped. During the previous bi-annual meeting, it was decided that more officers would be assigned to patrol the district of Bladestoke, which was particularly prone to burglary. In comparison to the other districts, such as Greyside, Blackmoore and Greenchapel, the number of burglaries in this district were astronomical. Since that meeting, burglary rates in the district, and as a whole, have dropped by over 5%. Police believe that the extra patrolling has had a knock-on effect to all of the other districts.

Finally, it was noted that there had been a sharp increase in the number of people caught speeding, between the hours of 12pm and 1am, since a camera was placed at the end of the motorway that joins South Ficshire and East Ficshire. This is a 10% rise from 9pm to 10pm, when the speed camera is also recording. The speed camera does not operate at any other times of the day, and is only active on Saturday nights.

17. Which is the most likely time for people to be caught speeding?

   a. 11pm – 1am, every night.

   b. 10pm – 11pm, Wednesday nights.

   c. 1am – 2am, Thursday nights.

   d. 12pm – 1am, Saturday nights.

18. Increasing patrols in which district, has improved burglary statistics in the others?

   a. Greyside.

   b. Blackmoore.

   c. Bladestoke.

   d. None of the above.

19. What could be done to decrease the murder rate in North Ficshire?

   a. Increase patrols between 1am and 2am, on Thursday nights.

   b. Increase patrols between 10pm and 11pm, every night.

   c. Increase patrols between 2pm and 3pm, every afternoon.

   d. Decrease patrols between 11am and 12pm, every morning.

Section Six

For the following questions, you need to read the four incidents carefully. You then need to decide, based purely on the information in these incidents, whether the perpetrator in Incident 4 can also be considered a suspect in Incidents 1, 2, and/or 3.

The 95th Precinct has been dealing with a rise in muggings over a few weeks. Three different incidents have taken place, with the following details for each:

Incident 1

Time and Date of Occurrence: 11:15pm on Thursday, September 14.

Place of Occurrence: Main Street.

Suspect Description: White male, early twenties, wearing a black tracksuit, black sneakers, and black cap. Suspect had brown eyes and brown hair.

Other Details: Suspect threatened victim with a knife and stole the victim's wallet.

Incident 2

Time and Date of Occurrence: 12:15am on Saturday, September 16.

Place of Occurrence: 19th Street.

Suspect Description: Black male, early twenties, wearing a black parka, blue jeans, and white sneakers. Suspect was bald, with brown eyes.

Other Details: Suspect used a knife to threaten the victim. Suspect stole a wallet and cell phone.

Incident 3

Time and Date of Occurrence: 8:55pm on Sunday, September 17.

Place of Occurrence: 19th Street.

Suspect Description: Black male, early thirties, wearing a black tracksuit and red sneakers. Suspect had short brown hair and was wearing sunglasses which concealed his eye color.

Other Details: Suspect used a handgun to threaten the victim. Suspect stole victims purse.

Four days later, the 95th Precinct made an arrest on an individual committing muggings:

Incident 4

Time and Date of Occurrence: Thursday, September 21.

Place of Occurrence: 13th Street.

Suspect Description: White male, early thirties, wearing a black tracksuit, black sneakers, and a black cap. Suspect had brown hair and green eyes.

Other Details: Suspect used a knife to threaten the victim. Suspect was arrested before they were capable of stealing anything from the victim.

---

20. The arrested person in Incident 4 can be considered a suspect in which of the following?

   a. Incident 1.

   b. Incident 2.

   c. Incident 3.

   d. None of the incidents.

Section Seven

For the following question type, you need to closely read and examine the four wanted posters over the next four pages. This is a form of memory test, so you will need to memorize the details of the images as well as the information beneath them. You have five minutes to read and examine all four of the wanted posters.

Once five minutes have passed, turn over and answer the questions based purely on the information that you have remembered from the wanted posters. You need to match the correct subject's image to the details in each question.

Subject 1

WANTED FOR LARCENY

Carey Carter

Age: 25

Eye Color: Brown.

Race: Black

Hair: Brown.

Height: 5'5"

Tattoo(s): None.

Weight: 130 pounds.

Scars: None.

Sex: Female

Subject wanted for stealing beauty products from a truck parked on 44th Street. Subject in known by police for previous attempts at theft. Subject is believed to have stolen approximately $400 worth of beauty products.

Subject 2

WANTED FOR MURDER

Tyler Burton

Age: 24

Eye Color: Green.

Race: White.

Hair: Blonde.

Height: 5'11".

Tattoo(s): None.

Weight: 150 pounds.

Scars: None.

Sex: Male.

Subject wanted for the murder of his girlfriend at her home on Valley Street. Subject used a shotgun during the murder, and is believed to be hiding somewhere within the city. The shotgun has been recovered.

Subject 3

WANTED FOR DRUG POSSESION

Austin Durrell

Age: 27   Eye Color: Brown.

Race: White.   Hair: Brown.

Height: 5'10".   Tattoo(s): None.

Weight: 160 pounds.   Scars: None.

Sex: Male.

Subject is wanted for possessing large quantities of cocaine and marijuana. Subject is known for loitering near high schools and on college campuses. It is believed that he intends to sell this product.

Subject 4

WANTED FOR ASSAULT

Max Tate

Age: 29

Race: White.

Height: 6'2".

Weight: 150 pounds.

Sex: Male.

Eye Color: Brown.

Hair: Brown.

Tattoo(s): None.

Scars: Surgery scars on right arm.

Subject assaulted a Hispanic male at a local shopping mall. Max has been known to write blog posts on the internet, often laced with racially-charged material.

21. Which of the subjects is known for loitering outside high schools and on college campuses?

    a. Subject One.

    b. Subject Two.

    c. Subject Three.

    d. Subject Four.

22. Which of the subjects has surgery scars on his left arm?

    a. Subject One.

    b. Subject Two.

    c. Subject Three.

    d. Subject Four.

23. Which of the subjects is wanted for assault?

    a. Subject One.

    b. Subject Two.

    c. Subject Three.

    d. Subject Four.

24. Which of the subjects is believed to be hiding in the city?

    a. Subject One.

    b. Subject Two.

    c. Subject Three.

    d. Subject Four.

Section Eight

For this section, read the information in each paragraph. Then, answer the three questions based purely on the information in the paragraph.

Officers in the 33rd Precinct have been researching local crime statistics over the last few weeks, in an attempt to tackle specific behaviour which has seen increased activity.

During their research, officers discovered that muggings occurred most frequently between 10pm and 1am every night. Shoplifting occurred most often during daytimes, between 1pm and 3pm on Mondays and Thursdays.

In addition, the research showed that assaults happened most frequently at night, between 8pm and midnight. Interestingly, car larceny most frequently occurred at the same time as assaults.

Finally, it was clear that carjacking was most often occurring on Saturday nights, between 7pm and 9pm.

25. In order to combat car larceny, which of the following patrols should be increased?

    a. 7pm to 9pm, every night.

    b. 8pm to midnight, every night.

    c. 9pm to midnight, every night.

    d. 10pm to 1am, every night.

26. In order to reduce shoplifting, which of the following patrols should be increased?

    a. 1pm to 3pm, on Mondays.

    b. 1pm to 3pm, every day.

    c. 2pm to 4pm, every day.

    d. 1pm to 3pm, on Mondays and Thursdays.

27. In order to reduce assaults, which of the following patrols should be increased?

a. 8pm to midnight, every night.

b. 8pm to 10pm, every night.

c. 1pm to 3pm, on Mondays and Thursdays.

d. 10pm to 1am, every night.

Section Nine

For each of the following questions, you will be given a series of information about a case. Once you've read it, choose the paragraph from the answer options which most accurately represents the information in the initial passage.

28. Detective Liza Harper has gathered the following facts during her investigation:

Place of Occurrence	Hank's Candy Store, Glass Avenue
Time of Occurrence	7:35pm
Time of Reporting	7:50pm, by a passer-by walking his dog.
Crime	Burglary
Victim(s)	N/A
Suspect	Male, white, early 20s
Weapon	Crowbar

Which of the following paragraphs best represents the above information?

a. A black male, in his early 20s, broke into a shop on Glass Avenue. After using a steel pipe to break in, he stole copious amounts of money from the cash register. A passer-by happened to notice this, and reported the incident to the police.

b. A white male, in his early 30s, broke into a candy shop on Glass Avenue. The burglary took place at 7:35pm. The suspect was noticed breaking into the store by a passer-by, who was walking his dog. The passer-by waited to see whether the man would steal anything, before reporting this incident to the police at 7:45pm.

c. A white male, in his early 20s, broke into Hank's Candy store on Glass Avenue at 7:35pm. The burglar used to crowbar to break through the door. A passer-by, who was walking his dog, noticed the alarm going off. He alerted the police at 7:50pm.

d. A black male, in his early 20s, broke into Hank's Candy store on Glass Avenue, at 7:38pm. He used a hammer to break through the store window. A passer-by noticed this, and immediately alerted the police as to what was happening, at 7:40pm.

Section Ten

For these questions, read the information in each passage. Then choose the most logical order for the information to appear in if you were writing a report.

Officer Michaels is writing a report concerning the discovery of a body. Her report consists of the following five sentences:

1. A short while later, at 9:50pm, the paramedics arrived. They immediately pronounced the man as dead.

2. Whilst I decided on the next steps, I was approached by two males, who claimed that the suspect was shot for 'snitching'. They blamed the police for his death.

3. I immediately made my way to the scene, where I discovered the body of a young male. He had been shot twice in the head, from close range.

4. At 9:35pm, I received a call from dispatch, informing me of a shooting on Lincoln Avenue.

5. Although the shooter has not yet been caught, police are making inroads into the murder, which is believed to be drug related.

29. Which order of the above sentences makes the most logical sense?

   a. 5, 2, 4, 3, 1.

   b. 5, 3, 1, 2, 4.

   c. 4, 3, 1, 2, 5.

   d. 4, 3, 2, 1, 5.

Answers to Mock Test 2

Section One

1. b = Kevin owing money to someone.

Explanation = This can be deduced since Officer Trueman informs his partner that Kevin owing money to someone is the most likely reason for the beating.

2. c = The passage strongly implies that Kevin was murdered by those whom he 'snitched on'.

Explanation = Next to Kevin's body was a note which read 'Snitch'. This strongly implies that Kevin was murdered by the people whom he informed on.

3. c = Thursday.

Explanation = The first paragraph reads that "It was now Thursday, and the officers had some serious questions to ask Kevin."

4. c = It is impossible to determine who attacked Kevin, based on the information given by the passage.

Explanation = The early passages, which discuss Kevin's attack, do not give any clear evidence as to who attacked him.

Section Two

5. c = Detective Bishop, shield #6362, narcotics investigation team.

Explanation = Field (10) is concerned with the name, shield number, and assignment of the detective assigned to the follow-up investigation. The final paragraph reads:

"Further investigation of the car by Detective Bishop (shield #6362), a member of the narcotics investigation team,"

6. a = Officer Weston.

Explanation = Field (8) is concerned with the arresting officer. The arresting officer in the passage is Officer Weston.

7. a = Michael Martinez.

Explanation = Field (1a) is concerned with the name of the first person arrested. The name of this person is Michael Martinez.

8. a = Shield #6432.

Explanation = Field (8a) is concerned with the shield number of the arresting officer. The arresting officer is Officer Weston, whose shield number is Shield #6432.

Section Three

9. c = Convertible.

Explanation = The third paragraph reads:

"Following this, the owner of the convertible apologised to Sergeant Pearson, and promised that she would fully cooperate with the police in any investigation that needed to be made."

10. d = Black.

Explanation = The sedan was the vehicle which drove away from the scene. The second paragraph states that the sedan was black.

11. a = Male.

Explanation = The third paragraph reads:

"The owner of the sedan then got back into his vehicle, and drove away."

12. d = Spoke to Sergeant Pearson's colleague.

Explanation = The final paragraph states:

"The woman who owned the van then approached Sergeant Pearson."

Section Four

13. a = 4.

Explanation = There are four cars on the road: three on the road closest to the camera, and another once on the perpendicular road straight away.

14. b = Left-hand side.

Explanation = The traffic light can be seen on the left-hand side of the crossing.

15. b = Café.

Explanation = The building on the right-hand side of the road has 'Café' written above it.

16. d = 2.

Explanation = There are two people playing musical instruments in the image. Both of them are on the left-hand side of the road: a guitarist, and an accordion player.

Section Five

17. d = 12am – 1am, Saturday nights.

Explanation = The final paragraph reads:

"Finally, it was noted that there had been a sharp increase in the number of people caught speeding, between the hours of 12pm and 1am..."

18. c = Bladestroke.

Explanation = The second paragraph states that it was decided to increase patrols in Bladestroke. This resulted in burglary dropping by 5% in it Bladestroke.

19. b = Increase patrols between 10pm and 11pm, every night.

Explanation = Murders happen most often between 10pm and 11pm. Therefore, increasing patrols in this time period would be most effective for reducing murders.

Section Six

20. d = None of the incidents.

Explanation = The description of the individual in Incident 4 does not match the description of suspects in the other incidents.

Section Seven

21. c = Subject Three.

Explanation = The wanted poster states that the subject loiters outside High Schools and on College Campuses.

22. d = Subject Four.

Explanation = The description of the subject on the wanted poster states that the subject has surgery scars on his left arm.

23. d = Subject Four.

Explanation = The wanted poster for Subject 4 states that they are wanted for assault.

24. b = Subject Two.

Explanation = The details in the wanted poster state that the subject is believed to be hiding somewhere in the city.

Section Eight

25. b = 8pm to midnight, every night.

Explanation = The third paragraph states that assaults and car larceny most frequently occurred at the same time, which is between 8pm and midnight.

26. d = 1pm to 3pm, on Mondays and Thursdays.

Explanation = The second paragraph states that shoplifting occurs most during daytime, between 1pm and 3pm on Mondays and Thursdays.

27. a = 8pm to midnight, every night.

Explanation = The third paragraph states that assaults occurred most frequently between 8pm and midnight, every night.

Section Nine

28. C = A white male, in his early 20s, broke into Hank's Candy store on Glass Avenue at 7:35pm. The burglar used to crowbar to break through the door. A passer-by, who was walking his dog, noticed the alarm going off. He alerted the police at 7:50pm.

Explanation = This paragraph includes all of the important information which is featured in the report, whilst the other answer options do not.

Section Ten

29. d = 4, 3, 2, 1, 5.

Explanation = When ordered as a paragraph, these statements read as:

"At 9:35pm, I received a call from dispatch, informing me of a shooting on Lincoln Avenue. I immediately made my way to the scene, where I discovered the body of a young male. He had been shot twice in the head, from close range. Whilst I decided on the next steps, I was approached by two males, who claimed that the suspect was shot for 'snitching'. They blamed the police for his death. A short while later, at 9:50pm, the paramedics arrived. They immediately pronounced the man as dead. Although the shooter has not yet been caught, police are making inroads into the murder, which is believed to be drug related."

THE POLICE
OFFICER INTERVIEW

The Police Officer Interview

At some point during the process of becoming a police officer, you will need to pass an interview. Whether this is before studying at police academy, during your studies, or just prior to graduation, you will need to sit in front of a panel of interviewers and answer a series of questions.

The focus of this chapter will be to give you material to help you prepare as much for the interview as possible. Like the entrance exam, it helps to have an idea about what questions you may be asked, so that you can answer them effectively. If you have a good idea about what questions are going to be asked, then you'll have time to prepare a model response to them.

In this chapter, we've supplied you with sample responses to a wide range of interview questions that you might be asked. While you aren't guaranteed to be asked all of these questions, it's likely that you will be asked to discuss similar ideas and experiences. Carefully read each sample response to get an understanding of what makes for an excellent answer.

After each sample response, we've supplied you with a space to write your own response. Remember to always think about how your own personal experiences relate to each question, but feel free to use the sample responses to get you in the correct frame of mind for each question.

Above all else, remember to be honest in your interview. You should *never* lie to the panel about your experiences, or even bend the truth to make things more convenient for you. Instead, take the time to think of honest responses which will portray you in the best light possible.

In addition to the sample police interview questions and answers, we've collected ten top tips for passing the police officer interview. Keep these in mind when thinking of your own answers to the interview questions.

Sample Police Interview Questions and Answers

SAMPLE INTERVIEW QUESTION 1

Q. Tell me about yourself and what qualities you believe you have, that will be relevant to the role of a police officer.

A. To begin with, I am a hard-working, committed and highly-motivated person who prides himself on the ability to continually learn and develop new skills. I am 31 years old, and I currently work as a customer services manager for a transportation company.

Prior to taking up this role approximately ten years ago, I spent five years working as a front-line soldier in the Army. In addition to being a family person, I also have my own hobbies and interests, which include team sports such as football and also playing the guitar in a local band.

I am a loyal person, who has a strong track record at work for being reliable, flexible and customer-focused. My annual appraisals are consistently to a high standard and I am always willing to learn new skills. Before applying for this job, I studied the role of a police officer and also the role of the police service in depth, to make sure I was able to meet the requirements of the role.

Having been working for my current employer for almost ten years now, I wanted to make sure that I had the potential to become a competent police officer before applying. Job stability is important to me and my family. If successful, I plan to stay in the police force for many years.

Finally, I believe that the additional qualities I possess would benefit the role of a police officer. These include being physically and mentally fit, organisationally and politically aware, determined, reliable, an excellent team player, organised, committed, capable of acting as a positive role model for the police force and being fully open to change.

YOUR OWN RESPONSE:

SAMPLE INTERVIEW QUESTION 2

Q. Why do you want to become a police officer and what made you decide to apply?

A. I have wanted to become a police officer for almost four years now, and I can distinctly remember the time I decided this would be the job for me. I was walking through my neighborhood on my way to the gym on an early Saturday morning, when I noticed two police officers dealing with an aggressive and verbally abusive young man who, from what I understood later on, had been caught shoplifting from the grocery store on the street.

Whilst walking past, I stopped a few yards on, to see how the police officers would handle the situation. The two police officers remained totally calm and in control of the situation, despite the abuse being directed at them by the man. Their body language was non-confrontational, and they appeared to be using well-thought out techniques to get him to calm down.

Once the man had calmed down, the officers arrested him and took him away in their police car. From that point on I wanted to learn more about the role of a police officer. I felt that, due to my previous experiences in the Armed Forces and also my natural abilities, I had what it takes to become a competent police officer.

I studied your website and also learnt all about the core competencies of the role. I then realised that I had the potential to become a police officer, and I have been waiting to apply ever since. In addition to this, I have lived in the local community for virtually all my life, and I feel proud that we live in a society that is, overall, safe and a great place to live.

I understand a large part of the role of being a police officer is reactive, but I would also be interested in working on the proactive and educational side of the job, whereby you get to educate the public to help keep them safe and also prevent crime from happening in the first place.

Finally, whilst I very much like my current job, and feel a debt of gratitude to my employer, I am very much ready for a new challenge and the next stage of my career. I believe I would be an excellent police officer if successful, and can assure you I would work hard to uphold the principles and the values the force expects from its employees.

YOUR OWN RESPONSE:

SAMPLE INTERVIEW QUESTION 3

Q. Tell me what work you have done during your preparation for applying to become a police officer.

A. I have carried out a huge amount of work, research and personal development on my journey to being here today. To begin with, I studied the role of a police officer, especially with regards to the core competencies. I wanted to make sure that I could meet the requirements of the role, so I asked myself whether I had sufficient evidence and experience to match each and every one of the core competencies.

Once I was certain that I had the experience in life, I started to find out more about the work the police carry out, both on a local and national level. I have studied your website in detail, and learnt as much as I possibly could about how you tackle crime, deal with the effects of it and also how you use statistics to drive down increasing crime trends in specific areas.

I have also briefly read some of the important policing policies you employ, such as the Operations and Partnership policy, the Human Resources policy and also the Professional Standards policy. Whilst I admit I did not read these in great detail, I wanted to make sure that I was prepared as possible for my interview today. In addition to reading and researching, I went along to my local police station to try and find out a bit more about the job, and the expectations that the public have from the police.

The police officer I spoke to was understandably very busy, but she did give me fifteen minutes of her time, whereby she explained what the job involved, what it was like working shifts and also the good points and challenging points about the job. After speaking with her, I felt I had a better understanding of the role and it only made me want to apply even more.

Finally, although I believe I am relatively fit, I started attending the gymnasium more to build up my physical strength and stamina. I also worked hard at increasing my times during the bleep test, and I can now get to level twelve since starting my application to join the police. I am very determined to become a police officer, and on that basis I have carried out lots of research to find out as much as I could about the role.

YOUR OWN RESPONSE:

SAMPLE INTERVIEW QUESTION 4

Q. If you witnessed a member of your team at work being verbally abused, what would you do?

A. First and foremost, I would intervene and stop it. Any type of abuse, both physical or verbal, should not be tolerated either in society or in the workplace. Everybody should feel safe at work and I believe I would have a responsibility as an employee to intervene.

Having said that, I would always make sure I followed the organisation's policy on bullying and harassment, and also follow the necessary reporting procedures required of me when dealing with such a situation. I would always remain calm and non-confrontational in a situation like this, and I would also take the opportunity to educate the offender on why their behaviour was not acceptable.

I would also speak to the person who was being verbally abused, to offer my support and to be on hand to listen to how they were feeling, following the abuse. Finally, I would report the situation to my line manager so that he or she could determine whether further action should be taken or not.

YOUR OWN RESPONSE:

SAMPLE INTERVIEW QUESTION 5

Q. What is the code of ethics employed by this police force?

A. Whilst studying your website, I did come across the code of ethics you employ and I decided to learn it. Basically, when any police officer or member of staff feels the standards within the force have not been met they can report their concerns to the Ethics Committee.

In addition to this, if any police officer or member of staff comes across a situation they feel unsure how to deal with, again they can raise this with the Ethics Committee. I would guess that the type of situation an officer might come across, whereby he or she were unsure how to deal with, would be if they attended a report of domestic abuse and a woman opened the door with a black eye. When the officer asks her what has happened, the woman says the child gave her the black eye by accident and then refuses to let them in.

I would guess this type of situation would be potentially difficult to deal with and the Ethics Committee could assist and advise if situations such as this arose again in the future. From what I understand, officers and staff have the option to remain anonymous after reporting any incident or situation to the Ethics Committee, if they so wish.

YOUR OWN RESPONSE:

SAMPLE INTERVIEW QUESTION 6

Q. What are the key priorities of this police force?

A. You currently have a large number of key priorities and these include cutting crime, catching criminals, dealing with anti-social behaviour, ensuring visible community policing is at the heart of everything you do, protecting the public from serious harm, providing a professional service by putting victims and witnesses first, meeting national commitments for policing, delivering value for money and also developing and supporting your workforce so they can do their job professionally and diligently.

NOTE: You should be able to find the key priorities for your chosen force on their website.

YOUR OWN RESPONSE:

SAMPLE INTERVIEW QUESTION 7

Q. We are interviewing forty people during the police officer final interviews, yet we only have vacancies for eighteen officers. What makes you better than the other applicants?

A. I believe I am the best candidate for this job for many reasons. First of all, I have been preparing for this role for many years now, by building up sufficient life experience and knowledge to be able to perform the role to a very high standard. Having studied all of the core competencies in detail, I feel I have plenty of experience to perform the duties of a police officer above and beyond the standards expected.

I am a flexible person who will be available to work at all times, whether its day or night and also at weekends. I have a supportive family who fully understand, appreciate and support my dream of becoming a police officer with this police force. In addition to knowing my strengths, I am also aware of the areas I need to work on in order to improve, and I have been working on these to make sure I am fully prepared for the police training course, if successful.

I have a good understanding and knowledge of the expectations that this police force expects from its staff, and I feel strongly that I will act as a good role model for the organisation that I am hoping to join. Finally, I understand that we live in times where the police force is under more scrutiny than ever and the requirement to be an employee who is open to and supportive of change has never been greater.

Once again, I feel strongly that I can adapt to a constantly changing environment, and provide the exceptional service that the public expects from its police officers. I can assure you that, if you give me the opportunity, I will not let you down and I will work harder than anyone to excel in the role.

YOUR OWN RESPONSE:

SAMPLE INTERVIEW QUESTION 8

Q. What are the standards of professional behaviour for this police force?

A. I did manage to locate and learn the standards of behaviour whilst studying your website. Whilst visiting my local police station to find out more about the role, the officer who showed me around and answered my questions, also mentioned how important these are. The standards are honesty and integrity, equality and diversity, use of force, authority, respect and courtesy, orders and instructions, duties and responsibilities, confidentiality, fitness for work, conduct and also challenging and reporting improper conduct. I understand these standards are very important to the role of a police officer, and I will ensure that I abide by them if successful.

YOUR OWN RESPONSE:

SAMPLE INTERVIEW QUESTION 9

Q. What are the objectives of this police force with regards to equality?

A. During my research, I managed to find out that the current equality objectives of your force are to work towards increasing the number of black and minority ethnic officers, to match that of the population in the county area. In addition to this, you are taking positive steps towards retaining and developing black and minority ethnic colleagues into specialist and supervisory roles.

NOTE: Each police force will have their own objectives with regards to equality. Please make sure you study the website of the police force that you are applying to join, in order to study their own equality policy.

YOUR OWN RESPONSE:

SAMPLE INTERVIEW QUESTION 10

Q. If a senior police officer told you to do something that you disagreed with, what would you do?

A. First and foremost I would obey his or her orders, as long as it was a lawful order. I understand I am joining a disciplined service, and it would be important that I followed their instructions.

Then, if after the incident or situation there was an opportunity for me to express my view in a respectful, positive and constructive manner, I would do so. I would always respect instructions and orders given to me, and perform any task to the highest possible standard.

YOUR OWN RESPONSE:

SAMPLE INTERVIEW QUESTION 11

Q. Do you think the police force provides value for money to the public? If so, why?

A. Absolutely, one-hundred percent I believe the police force offers value for money. Whilst I very much want to become a police officer and work within the force, I too live in the local community and I have only seen great things from the police.

From what I can see on a local level in my community, the police work very hard to educate the public and reduce crime, despite having limited resources. I understand that the police force budget has been reduced over recent years, yet despite this, your website shows that the force is becoming more efficient in tackling crime than ever before.

For example, your force has managed to reduce vehicle related crime by seventeen percent over the last twelve months. I was very impressed by those statistics. I would imagine that, whilst the media and press can be very helpful in helping the police to catch offenders and reduce crime, sometimes the police can be painted in a negative light by them.

On that basis, I would imagine it would be part of my job as a police officer to act as a positive role model for the police and work hard to educate the public about the good work the force is doing and demonstrate value for money is being delivered.

YOUR OWN RESPONSE:

SAMPLE INTERVIEW QUESTION 12

Q. You are attending a local school talking to the children about the work of the police force. The teacher asks you to explain to the children how to call 911 in an emergency. What would you tell them?

A. I would tell them that they should only call 911 if it is an emergency. I would then give them examples of when to call 911, including if a crime is happening right now, someone is in immediate danger, there is a risk of serious damage to property, a suspect for a serious crime is nearby, or there is a traffic collision involving injury or danger to other road users. I would then use the opportunity to educate the children on why it is important they do not make hoax calls under any circumstances, as this could block the telephone lines for someone who really does need the police or other emergency services. I would then tell the children that the police do have an alternative number they can call if it is a non-emergency. The number they would need in a non-emergency situation is 311, and I would then give them additional examples of non-emergency situations, such as reporting a crime not currently in progress, giving information to the police about crime in their area, speaking to the police about a general enquiry and also contacting a specific police officer or member of staff. Finally, I would then ask the children if any of them had any questions to make sure they understood the information I had provided them with.

212 Police Officer Exam

YOUR OWN RESPONSE:

SAMPLE INTERVIEW QUESTION 13

Q. Can you give an example of when you have challenged inappropriate behaviour in a working environment?

A. Yes, I can. I currently work as an IT consultant and I was carrying out contract work for a large corporate company upstate. I was having a coffee break on my own in the company canteen, when I overheard a man verbally abusing a female colleague. I immediately went over to the man and said in a calm and respectful manner that I found his comment to be offensive, and requested that he didn't use that type of language, as it is unwelcome.

I could sense he was angered by my comments, and he proceeded to tell me to mind my own business. I remained calm, and reiterated my request, by asking him once again not to use that type of offensive language in the workplace. I stated that, if he continued to use that type of language, I would report him to the company Managing Director. He immediately changed his tone, apologised and then got up and left the canteen.

I then spoke to the lady whom the comment was directed at and explained the reasons why I had intervened. She told me she was grateful for my interaction and said that he often spoke to her in that manner. To my amazement, she informed me that the man who made the comment was in fact her line manager. After I left the canteen, I sent an email directly to the Managing Director of the company informing her of what I had just witnessed in the canteen, whilst also explaining what I had done to prevent it from happening again. I would never hesitate to challenge any type of behaviour that was either inappropriate, bullying in nature or discriminatory. This type of behaviour is not acceptable and should be challenged.

YOUR OWN RESPONSE:

SAMPLE INTERVIEW QUESTION 14

Q. You are a serving police officer and you are on foot patrol in the local main street on a busy Friday night. The time is 11pm, and a member of public runs up to you and tells you that a fight has just started in the bar opposite. You look over to the bar and you can see the fight has already spilled out into the road. From what you can see, there appears to be a group of at least ten men fighting. Whilst I understand you are not a serving police officer, tell me what you think you would do in this type of situation?

A. To begin with, I would make sure that I followed my training and the operational procedures I would have learnt during my training course and tutoring. I would act fast, whilst remaining calm and in control and the safety of the public would be my number one priority. I would make a rapid assessment of the scene, before calling the control centre to request back up.

I would make my way over to the scene whilst shouting out to the group of men that the police were now in attendance and they were to stop fighting. I would make my observations regarding which men were involved, including taking a mental note of what they looked like and what clothes they were wearing.

I would tell everyone who was not involved in the fight to stay in the pub or stay a safe distance away from the scene. Then, if safe to do so, I would try to break up the fight and arrest any individuals involved.

Once back up arrived, I would request that the attending officers assist with arresting further individuals involved in the fight, and also with taking statements from witnesses. Finally, once the scene was safe, I would speak to the manager of the bar to see if the CCTV had picked up the incident.

The footage from any CCTV images captured would allow me to build a picture as to why the fight happened and also who was involved. At all times I would focus on safety, and also make sure that I followed my training and operational procedures.

YOUR OWN RESPONSE:

SAMPLE INTERVIEW QUESTION 15

Q. What type of work do you think you will be undertaking as a police officer, if you are successful?

A. I believe the work I would undertake will be extremely diverse and varied in nature, and that the role would require me to use a wide remit of skills and expertise. To begin with, I would be acting as a positive role model for the police force, by behaving with honesty and integrity; and delivering a service to the public that exceeds their expectations.

I would also be providing, on a daily basis, a reassuring high-visibility presence within the community, whilst also responding to incidents, gathering evidence and taking contemporaneous notes and statements of incidents and reports of crimes as and when they are reported. I would be required to attend and protect crime scenes, and also investigate incidents through effective policing and by also following my training and operational procedures at all times.

I would make arrests when appropriate, complete custody procedures and also interview suspects and present evidence in court. I would liaise and work with other stakeholders and agencies, to make sure that we all worked towards the common goal of protecting the community in which we serve. I would also be required to put vulnerable people, victims of crime and witnesses first.

I would be required to face challenging and difficult situations on a daily basis, and I would need to be at my best at all times to ensure I uphold the principles of policing. Finally, I would be required to adopt the core competencies of the police officer's role, and utilise interpersonal skills to diffuse and respond with integrity in any situation.

YOUR OWN RESPONSE:

SAMPLE INTERVIEW QUESTION 16

Q. How can we, as a local police force, improve relations with the local community?

A. I think there are a number of different ways you can improve relations. I am sure you do many of these things already, but promoting all of the good work you do within the community via the local press will help to demonstrate to the public that the good work you are doing is making a difference to their lives.

I also feel that working closely with community groups and community leaders can be a positive thing, to demonstrate that the police force is listening to people's concerns and issues. I also think that it is very important that the police follow up and keep people updated with progress on policing matters. For example, if the police hold community meetings where local residents are encouraged to share their concerns, somebody must follow up with a progress report or communicate what work has been done to deal with their concerns, if they are a policing-related matter.

I would also imagine that it is my responsibility as a police officer, if I am to be successful, to be as visible as possible within the community. It would be my job to speak to people and reassure them that the police are there to serve them and provide a reassuring presence. I also feel that relations with the police has to start at an early age. I understand budgets must be very restricted, but if police officers are able to attend schools and talk to children from an early age about the type of work they do, that can only be a good thing and it will help to give the children a positive impression of the police from an early age.

Community policing, I would imagine, means working proactively and building relationships in the face of tension and issues. So, if there are problems within a particular area that I am serving in, it would be my job to help ease those tensions and build better relationships with the community by working alongside community leaders. I guess the police service would cease to function without the active support of the communities it serves. Effective community engagement, targeted foot patrols, and collaborative problem solving would significantly increase public confidence in policing activity.

YOUR OWN RESPONSE:

SAMPLE INTERVIEW QUESTION 17

Q. How do you keep yourself physically fit?

A. I take personal responsibility for my fitness and I fully understand how important this would be to my role as a police officer. At present, I go running four times a week in the mornings before I start work. I like to get up early and get my fitness routine out of the way, which then leaves me time to spend with my family once I get home from work.

I usually run five kilometers each time, and this ensures my body fat is kept to a healthy level and my concentration levels are at their peak. My current job involves me having to concentrate for long periods of time and I have a responsibility to make sure I can perform at work to a high standard.

On weekends, I spend time playing hockey for a local team. We are not overly competitive; however, I like the fact I get to play a team sport and interact with other people from the community. We also go out together socially once a month and I really enjoy that side of being part of a hockey team.

YOUR OWN RESPONSE:

SAMPLE INTERVIEW QUESTION 18

Q. Can you tell me about a time when you have gathered information from a wide range of sources before making a difficult decision?

A. Actually, I was involved in a situation of this nature quite recently. Whilst at work it came to my attention that a colleague was not pulling his weight. In addition to not doing his job properly, there had been a couple of times whereby I could smell alcohol on his breath. I was naturally concerned for his welfare and also concerned for the fact that other team members were starting to get frustrated with his lack of performance within the team.

Our line manager was away on holiday for two weeks, so I decided to see if I could do anything to stop this situation from deteriorating any further. I also wanted to see if I could resolve this issue before my line manager returned to work. Whilst I would still need to report my concerns to my line manager when she got back, I wanted to do all I could to get to the bottom of this, as it was starting to affect the team. I thought carefully about the actions that I was going to take, and decided that the best course of action would be to gather as much information as possible from a variety of sources.

Before speaking to my colleague about his work issues and the smell of alcohol, I wanted to ask my other colleagues within the team whether any of them were aware that our colleague was having problems at home. It's sometimes far too easy to jump into a situation, and start accusing someone of wrongdoing without first of all gathering the facts. After speaking to members of my team, it became apparent that our colleague was suffering from depression.

Apparently, his girlfriend of eight years had run off with his friend, and he was finding things very difficult to deal with. This, in turn, was starting to have a negative impact on his personal and working life and he was allegedly turning to alcohol in order to drown his sorrows. Because of the seriousness of the situation, I then decided to speak to our Human Resources department before sitting down with my work colleague to see what types of support were available for people in his situation.

As it transpires, our organisation offers free counselling for people who need it, but the referral would need to come from our line manager first. At this stage I felt I had sufficient background information to speak to our work colleague who was underperforming. I think that, without carrying out my research and gathering the background information that I now had, I could have quite easily made the situation worse by criticising our colleague because of his under-performance at work and the smell of alcohol on his breath.

With the information I had, I would now take an entirely different approach when speaking to him. I asked my colleague to come and sit with me during tea break in quiet room where we would not be disturbed. I explained to him that I was genuinely worried for him and that I wanted to help him out. I asked him if he wanted to talk to me about anything at all and I reassured him that whatever he told me would be treated with confidence. Before he could even say anything, his eyes filled up and he started to cry. I put my arms around him and told him not to worry and that everything would be fine.

After a short while, he started to talk and told me about the situation he was in with regards to his girlfriend of eight years running off with his friend. He went on to explain that he was drinking heavily at night to get over the pain. I listened to him carefully and then decided to take control of the situation by making some positive suggestions that were designed to help him.

I asked for his permission to speak to our line manager so that we could get him some help through the counselling service the organisation offered. Thankfully, he agreed to give this a try. I told him that, as soon as our line manager returned to work, I would ask her to start the referral process for getting him some much-needed counselling. Finally, I gave him my mobile telephone number and said that we should speak every day until our line manager returned to work.

I explained how I would be there to support him through this difficult time and that I would be there to listen at any time, day or night. Whilst this situation was very difficult to deal with, especially due to its sensitive nature, I felt that by gathering all of the facts first it gave me the opportunity to make the right decisions and ultimately take the right course of action.

YOUR OWN RESPONSE:

Further Interview Questions to Prepare For

Q. Are you an organised person? If you are, give me an example of when you have been highly organised in a work environment.

Q. What are the different ranks of the uniformed police service?

Q. Can you give an example of when you have made a difficult decision whilst working under pressure?

Probing question 1: What difficulties did you face whilst working under pressure?

Probing question 2: Would you do anything different if the same 'working under pressure' situation arose again?

Q. Can you tell me about a time when you have worked in partnership with others to solve a problem?

Q. Which parts of the police officer job do you think you'll like the most?

Q. Which parts of the police officer job do you think you'll dislike the most?

Q. Can you tell me about a time when you have had to defuse a conflict situation?

Q. Can you give me an example of when you have delivered outstanding customer service?

Q. Have you discussed your application to the police force with your friends and do you have the support of your family?

Q. Can you give an example of when you have demonstrated flexibility in the workplace?

Q. If you are unsuccessful at this attempt, what would you do?

Don't forget, the interview questions and sample responses that I have provided are not guaranteed to be the exact questions you will get asked during your interview. However, they will be a great basis on which to start your preparation. In addition to using this guide, please do make sure you carry out your own research both online and offline, and try to come up with your own anticipated interview questions prior to your interview.

Police Officer Interview Tips and Advice

Here are our top ten tips for passing the police officer interview from interivew expert Richard McMunn. Each tip is then immediately followed by a brief narrative, explaining what the tip is, and why I believe it to be important.

Success is in Your Hands, Nobody Else's

Before you start preparing for the final interview, remember that the amount of preparation you put into the interview can have an impact on the result. I truly believe that success is in your hands, and nobody else's.

I have heard some pathetic excuses in my time, for why some people believe they failed the police selection process. The one excuse that I hear time and again is this one:

"I didn't get in because the police are only looking for women, and they don't want white males."

This is complete nonsense. Yes, the police force is actively looking to recruit people from under-represented groups (and rightly so, too), but that does not mean you won't get in because you are not from an under-represented group. Just focus on getting the highest scores possible during the final interview, and you will be successful.

Sometimes in life we have to try very hard to get what we want. Sometimes in life we have to keep persevering, even when we fail the first time around. Although the following short story has no relevance to you joining the police force, I wanted to share a personal experience of mine, which I had at the age of 16. This had a significant impact on way that I tackle setbacks in my life.

When I was a teenager (16), I tried to join the Royal Navy. I failed the medical because I was a stone overweight. I can remember leaving the medical at the doctor's surgery, and I was both gutted and humiliated. However, instead of giving up and moaning about my situation, I started running and I also drastically improved my diet. After a month of intense training and improved eating, I applied to join the Royal Navy again; only this time I passed. The reason I failed the first time around was down to me, and conversely the reason why I passed the second time was also down to me. Take responsibility for your own success in life – work hard, continually look for ways to improve and success will come your way.

Be Someone Who Embraces Change

Working in the public sector is different to how it used to be. When I joined many years ago, we didn't really care much for change. The old adage of "if it ain't broke don't fix it" was often heard being said in the workplace. This attitude and approach to working life does not cut it anymore.

The pressure on public sector organizations such as the police force has never been as intense as it is today, and this pressure will only increase as the years go by. As such, the police force needs people who will not only support change, but also embrace it.

During your preparation, make sure you are able to provide examples of where you have supported and promoted change in the workplace. This is very important.

Take Responsibility for Your Own Health and Fitness

The responsibility to maintain fitness as a police officer rests with you. A police officer should be able to climb walls and run after/tackle criminals. If they are unable to meet the demands of the job, then unfit police officers could put themselves, their colleagues, and the general public in danger.

As a police officer you could find yourself in a situation whereby you are required to wear heavy protective equipment whilst tackling mobs during a riot. It is times like this where you will be tested both physically and mentally, and you will need to make sure that you are capable of performing your duties both competently and professionally.

The good news is, you do not need to be mega fit to join the police force. In my view, the fitness standards are set quite low. I would be surprised if you don't get asked a question at the interview that explores what you do in your spare time, and also how you keep yourself physically fit and active.

Be "Politically" Aware

What do I mean by this? Well, in a nutshell, it means understanding that the police service is exactly that: a service. The police service is not only responsible to the members of the public whom it serves, but it is also responsible to the Government that is in power at that particular time.

The Government will generally have a large say in how the police force operates, and on that basis, things can change very quickly from time to time. That is one of the reasons why the police service is keen to employ people who are capable of and willing to accept change.

We have all been in jobs before where some of the longest-serving employees have become "dinosaurs". These people are often unhelpful, obstructive and unwilling to accept or embrace change. Don't become one of them, as they are not pleasant to work with. When you join the police force, be willing to embrace change, regardless of how long you have served.

Carry out a Practice Interview

Trust me, this will really help to boost your confidence before you walk into the interview room. The police officer final interview will be one of the most important interviews you will ever attend. Therefore, you should do all you can to be at your peak on the day.

One of the best tips I can give you is to carry out at least one mock interview before your big day (preferably three or four!). A mock interview involves asking a friend or relative to sit down in front of you and ask you all of the questions contained within this chapter.

The final interview will probably last for approximately 60 minutes; therefore, you have to be capable of doing the majority of talking for that length of time. Don't let the first time that you answer the questions I have provided within this guide be at the actual interview itself. You want your answers to the questions to flow, and the only way you will achieve this is by practising your answers before the real thing.

Provide Lots of Evidence when Answering the Interview Questions

Evidence, evidence, evidence. If you have got this far in the selection process, you will have already demonstrated your ability to provide answers to competency-based interview questions at the assessment centre interview.

Don't be fooled into thinking you won't need to provide further evidence during the final interview, because you will. Make sure you have sufficient evidence to offer the panel, for all of the core competencies that are required of the role of police officer.

In addition to this, and as part of your study, make sure you prepare answers to the "additional" interview questions, which I have included towards the end of this guide. There are a number of situational questions contained within that particular part. Finally, when answering situational interview questions, use the STAR technique for structuring your responses:

Situation – What was the situation you were in?

Task – What was the task that you and others had to carry out, and what difficulties did you have to overcome along the way?

Action – What action did you and others take whilst carrying out the task? (Tip: when responding to "team-related" situational interview questions, refer to the team as "we", as opposed to "I".

Result – What was the result following yours and the team's actions?

Finally, at the end of your response, tell the interview panel what you LEARNED from the process and what, if anything, you would do differently next time.

Have a Thorough Understanding of the Role of a Police Officer, and also the Role of the Police Force

You don't need me to tell you that you should have a thorough understanding of the role of a police officer, and also the role of the police force, before you attend your interview.

However, you would be amazed at how many people get caught out by simple questions such as:

> **"Tell me what you would expect to be doing on a day-to-day basis as a police officer."**

and

> **"What is the primary role of the police force and what, exactly, are our objectives?"**

Whilst I will go into more detail during tip number 10 about not getting caught out by easy questions, do make sure you know exactly what the role of a police officer and the police force is.

Be Prepared to Ask the Panel Two Questions at the end of the Interview

At the end of the interview, it is good practice to ask a couple of questions, if invited to do so.

At the end of the sample interview questions and answers section of this guide, I have provided two sample questions that you might consider asking. However, I also think it's good practice to come up with a couple of your own. Just make sure that, whatever questions you do ask, they are intelligent and they are not designed to catch the interview panel out or make you look clever.

Don't Get Caught out at the Start of the Interview!

More often than not, it can be the "easy" questions that we find the hardest to answer. Questions such as 'Why do you want to be a police officer?' and 'What areas do you most need to improve on?' can often catch us off guard. Therefore, make sure you prepare just as much for the easy questions as for the harder situational-type questions. To help you prepare in this area, here are some tips:

- Consider what you do well (what are you good at?);

- Consider which areas you need to develop or which areas do you need to work on. (In particular, are there any aspects of the initial recruit training course you might find difficult or challenging?);

- Assess your strengths and development areas (what are you doing to improve on your development areas, especially in your current job?);

- Consider what is important to you;

- Consider what you find challenging;

- Review how others may perceive you (be prepared to answer truthfully about how other people perceive you and take steps to improve in areas that need development. Remember, police officers should act with integrity and honesty at all times).

A FEW FINAL WORDS...

You have now reached the end of your guide to the USA Police Officer tests, and no doubt you feel more prepared to tackle the police officer entrance exam. We hope you have found this guide an invaluable insight into the test, and understand the expectations regarding your assessment.

For any type of test, we believe there are a few things to remember in order to better your chances and increase your overall performance.

REMEMBER – THE THREE Ps!

Preparation. This may seem relatively obvious, but you will be surprised by how many people fail their assessment because they lacked preparation and knowledge regarding their test. You want to do your utmost to guarantee the best possible chance of succeeding. Be sure to conduct as much preparation prior to your assessment to ensure you are fully aware and 100% prepared to complete the test successfully. Not only will practising guarantee to better your chances of successfully passing, but it will also make you feel at ease by providing you with knowledge and know-how to pass your Law National Admissions Test.

Perseverance. You are far more likely to succeed at something if you continuously set out to achieve it. Everybody comes across times whereby they are setback or find obstacles in the way of their goals. The important thing to remember when this happens, is to use those setbacks and obstacles as a way of progressing. It is what you do with your past experiences that helps to determine your success in the future. If you fail at something, consider 'why' you have failed. This will allow you to improve and enhance your performance for next time.

Performance. Your performance will determine whether or not you are likely to succeed. Attributes that are often associated with performance are *self-belief, motivation* and *commitment.* Self-belief is important for anything you do in life. It allows you to recognise your own abilities and skills and believe that you can do well. Believing that you can do well is half the battle! Being fully motivated and committed is often difficult for some people, but we can assure you that, nothing is gained without hard work and determination. If you want to succeed, you will need to put in that extra time and hard work!

Good luck with your police officer entrance exam. We wish you the best of luck with all your future endeavours!

The how2become team

The How2Become Team

FOR MORE CAREERS GUIDANCE GO TO:

WWW.HOW2BECOME.COM

Made in the USA
Middletown, DE
07 July 2018